SAINT
JOHN
BOSCO

*"And taking a child, he set him in the midst
of them. Whom when he had embraced, he saith
to them: Whosoever shall receive one such child
as this in my name, receiveth me. And whosoever shall receive me, receiveth not me, but him
that sent me."*

—Mark 9:35-36

St. John Bosco

SAINT JOHN BOSCO

1815-1888

THE FRIEND OF YOUTH

FOUNDER OF THE SALESIAN SOCIETY,
OF THE SISTERS OF MARY, HELP OF CHRISTIANS,
AND OF THE SALESIAN CO-OPERATORS

By

F. A. Forbes

"And he was a stout hunter before the Lord."
—Genesis 10:9

TAN BOOKS AND PUBLISHERS, INC.
Rockford, Illinois 61105

Imprimi Potest: August Bosio, S.D.B.
                 Provincial Superior

Nihil Obstat: Thomas Comber
                 Censor Deputatus

Imprimatur: ✝ Joseph P. Hurley, D.D.
                 Bishop of St. Augustine
                 April 9, 1941

ISBN 0-89555-663-4

Library of Congress Control No.: 00-131565

Cover and frontispiece illustrations courtesy of the Salesian Society.

Printed and bound in the United States of America.

TAN BOOKS AND PUBLISHERS, INC.
P.O. Box 424
Rockford, Illinois 61105
2000

Da mihi animas; tolle ceteras.
"Give me souls; take away the rest."
—St. John Bosco

CONTENTS

1. The Making of an Apostle 1
2. The Mending of a Broken Hope 19
3. The Tempering of the Steel 38
4. The Dream Fulfilled 58
5. A Mighty Enterprise 80
6. The Ways of a Saint 104
7. "Ask and You Shall Receive" 130
8. The Saving Cross 155
9. The Great Achievement 179
10. The Spread of the Work 201

FOREWORD

THIS LIFE, so full of color and of drama, will appeal to all, whatever their creed or opinions.

St. John Bosco, or simply "Don Bosco," as he wished to be called, spent himself wholly, from his very childhood, in healing modern human miseries. As he saw and foresaw the dangerous surging tide of misled popular masses longing for justice, he threw himself headlong among the youth of the lower classes, pointing to them the only way to a better place in this life and in the life to come.

He did not talk much: he acted. He did not write long and elaborate educational treatises: his example is the best one. When asked about the secret of his immense success with the youngsters, he simply answered: "love . . ."

By a kind of surprising intuition, Don Bosco knew that selfishness, bearing injustice and hatred, was at the bottom of this modern society, forever prattling about equality, philanthropy and fraternity. He felt the sting of the sarcasm and of the tragedy of the common people proclaimed "sovereign" in theory, but in fact reduced to slavery by this blustering modern liberalism, which raised the flickering torch of human "reason" against the eternal light. Don Bosco set himself to bring back the multitudes to the only "Heart" that understood their needs. He is the greatest pioneer of Christ in modern times.

This book is the fruit of gratitude, the loving "Thank you" for a great favor miraculously granted to the author through Don Bosco's intercession. The reader will feel the throbbing of a grateful heart in every page.

As to its veracity, suffice it to state that Don Bosco's figure stands out vividly against the background of the latter part of the 19th century.

May this book carry far and wide through our beloved country the old and always new Spirit of Christ as the only remedy for the ailments of this suffering age!

SAINT JOHN BOSCO

"Suffer the little children to come unto me, and forbid them not; for of such is the kingdom of God."

—Mark 10:14

Chapter 1

THE MAKING OF AN APOSTLE

ST. JOHN BOSCO'S mother, like the mother of many great men, was a notable woman, one of the heroic company of Catholic wives and mothers who carry the great ideals of their faith into the smallest things of life. Margaret Occhiena was a native of Capriglio, a little village among the vine-clad hills of Piedmont in the neighborhood of Turin. In early womanhood she married Francis Bosco, a young widower, who farmed his tiny property in the neighborhood hamlet of Becchi. Francis Bosco had a son by his first marriage, a boy of nine, Anthony, and he had taken his old mother to live with him. Margaret took the motherless boy and the old woman to her heart and made the little household a real home.

Joseph, her eldest son, was born in 1813, John two years later. The little family was very happy in spite of poverty, until, scarcely two years after the birth of John, Francis Bosco died of a sudden attack of pneumonia. Little John never forgot how his mother took him into the room where his father lay very still on the bed. She was leading him out again when he pulled back, crying that he wanted to "stay with father." Margaret burst into tears. "My little John, you no longer have a father," she said, and a strange chill fell upon the heart of the child.

It was an uphill fight, now that the bread-winner was gone, but Margaret set herself bravely to the task of providing for the household. There was much work to be done at Becchi, and the boys were taught to work hard. At four years old, little John was already doing his share, tending the cattle, gathering sticks for the fire, or watching the bread his mother had put down to bake. They lived hard too—up with the dawn in winter and summer, a slice of dry bread for breakfast, and off with a cheerful face to whatever the day's work might be.

Margaret Bosco, though herself unlearned, was a born educator. The beginning and end of her teaching was God. Morning and evening the whole household knelt together, asking their daily bread, both for soul and body, for courage to do well, and pardon for what was done less well. Margaret seldom punished. "God always sees you," she used to say, "even when I do not. I may not be there, but He is always there." She would speak to her children of His beauty, revealed in the lovely world of His creation, and when their tiny vineyard, as sometimes happened, was stripped of its fruit by a sudden hailstorm: "God gave them to us," she would say, "and He has taken them away. He is the Master; may His Will be done." And when in the winter evenings they sat by the fire, listening to the wind that howled around the little cottage, "Children," she would say, "let us thank God, who is so good to us. He is truly a Father— our Father in Heaven." When the children were tempted to be untruthful: "Take care," she would say, "God sees our most secret thoughts"—and out would come the truth.

Those were terrible years of war and famine in Italy. Beggars of all description went from village to village seeking food, and it was noticed that even though Margaret herself might be in need, no one ever went hungry from her door, nor was any wanderer refused shelter. If anyone in the hamlet was sick and needing wine or food, however low might be her own little store, she would give what she had.

Anthony, John's stepbrother, was a difficult boy, surly and ill-tempered. Though Margaret always treated him with respect as eldest of the family and loved him as her own son, he was always ready to think that the other two were being treated better than he, though in his heart he knew better. It was through the patient tenderness and forbearance, as well as the wise teaching of Margaret Bosco, that this most trying of her children grew up later into a good and upright man.

Little John was by far the most intelligent of the three, and though full of life and vigor, the most responsive to her teaching. He loved to help his mother in her charitable actions; when she went to visit a sick neighbor he went with her, and while she attended to the invalid, he would gather the children around him and teach them their prayers. Wherever he was he was the leader, in games as in everything else, and even as a child of five he used his influence for good. Sometimes his mother would object to his choosing the roughest boys to play with, especially when he came home rather the worse for wear. John would coax her—"You see, Mother, when I play with them, they are not so nasty, they don't fight and use bad words." It was quite true. There was a radiant purity about the child that influenced all with whom he came in contact.

Through all the earlier years of his life, little John herded the cattle. He led them out joyously into the meadow, singing one of the hymns to Our Lady that his mother had taught him. The silence and beauty of the open country led his thoughts to God; he became a lover of silence and prayer. The little shepherds of the neighborhood, with whom he was very popular, sometimes interrupted him, and he would tell them a story or repeat part of the last catechism lesson of his mother. And he had such a delightful way of doing it that they came again and again. Among them was a poor little fellow who had only a hunk of black bread for his breakfast. "I'd like your bread better than mine," said John one day. "Will you trade?" He had a large slice of good white bread such as Margaret always provided for her children; little Matteo was ready enough to trade, but he thought John had very strange likings. The exchange continued daily, and it was only after many years that it struck Matteo that liking had not had much to do with it.

When John was about nine, it became evident to his mother that he was destined for something other than a shepherd's life. There was no school at Murialdo, the nearest village; and Castelnuovo, where there was one, was a good distance away. There would be some expense. Anthony, now 20, consulted as the head of the family, put his foot down firmly. "He can dig like the rest of us," he said. "I have never been to school." Margaret, rather than cause any trouble in the home, gave way. But her sister, housekeeper to the parish priest at Capriglio, who acted also as a schoolmaster, begged him to take the child as pupil in the class which began in early November and ended with the spring. The little scholar had to tramp three miles twice a day in all weather, but he thought it a cheap price to pay and quickly learned to read. During the spring and summer, when at work in the fields again, he studied whenever he had a free moment and while herding the cattle.

"I want to study, I want to be a priest," he would reply to the rather violent remonstrances of his young friends. With the return of winter there was a question of going back to the class at Capriglio, but again Anthony turned crusty, and again Margaret thought it better not to insist.

During his whole life John Bosco was to be inspired and guided by strangely vivid dreams, God's revelation of what his work in the world was to be. The first took place about this time when he was nine years old. He seemed to be in a large yard near the cottage, where a great many boys were playing together; some were laughing, some playing games, some fighting, some swearing and using foul language. John shouted to them to stop and, dashing in, began to strike at them. Suddenly, by his side, he was aware of a shining figure in white, of unparalleled dignity and with a face so radiant that he could not bear to look at it.

"Not with blows, but with gentleness and charity, you must take care of them and win their hearts," he said, "teach them the beauty of virtue and the ugliness of sin."

"How can I teach them, who am ignorant myself?" asked John.

"By obedience and knowledge, you will do the impossible," was the answer.

"How can I get knowledge?"

"I will give you the wisest of teachers; she will teach you true knowledge."

"Who are you who speak thus to me?"

"I am the Son of her whom your mother has taught you to salute three times a day."

"My mother has also taught me to be careful of strangers. What is your name?"

"Ask My Mother."

At that moment John saw beside his interlocutor a beautiful Lady clothed like her Son in shining raiment. She took him by the hand. "Look," she said. The boys had vanished, and in their place he saw a crowd of wild animals.

"This is your work," she said. "Be humble and strong. I will show you now what you must do with my children."

As she spoke the animals vanished, and in

their place he saw lambs gamboling and frisking about the Lady and her Son. John began to cry, "What does it mean?" The lady laid a gentle hand on his head. "You will understand later," she said, and John awoke. He slept no more that night.

So that was to be his work—to teach the beauty of goodness and the ugliness of sin. How was he to do it? Little John had an idea. The great entertainments in those days in Italy were the performances of the traveling jugglers and acrobats who were always to be seen on market days in the villages and towns. It had not escaped John's keen eyes that people would even stay away from church to look at them. From henceforth, whenever a juggler was to be seen, there was John watching. Then he went home and practiced. He was black and blue for a while, but he was a supple little fellow and soon he began to get the knack of it.

Before very long, he had acquired most of the tumbler's tricks and could even walk on a tightrope rigged up between two trees—not too far from the ground. Then he planned his program. The children of the neighborhood were invited to a performance, only it was prefaced and ended by prayer, and somewhere in the middle John gave them what he could remember of the Sunday sermon, all with the inimitable energy and spirit that was his. It was made quite clear from the beginning that "No prayers, no performance" was to be the order of the day, and John was inexorable on this point. It was for their souls' welfare that he had been black and blue all over, not to give them a pleasant afternoon. To the circle of admirers it was as good as a first-class circus, and they never failed to appear. They were intensely proud of John.

At ten years old John Bosco made his First Communion. In those days, before the happy pronouncement of Saint Pius X, children did not approach the Holy Table until about 12 or 13. But Margaret Bosco, understanding all that it would mean for her little son, sent him to the preparatory class at Castelnuovo in the Lent of 1826. Though younger than all the rest, he was the most understanding, as well as the one who knew his catechism the best. Margaret herself prepared him for the great act. "My little son," she said, "God is about to give you the most precious of His gifts. Make ready your whole soul to receive Him and promise Him to be faithful to Him all your life." On the morning of the great day she herself took him to the church at Castelnuovo and they made their Communion together. The Master entered into lasting possession of the soul of His young servant.

John had told his mother of his dream, and

to her it seemed a clear indication that he was
meant for the priesthood. Yet there was Anthony's
savage opposition to his little brother's education to be dealt with. She commended it to God,
and God heard her prayer. That year, in honor
of the Jubilee of 1826, an eight days' mission
was held in the towns and larger villages of Piedmont. Buttigliera being nearer than Castelnuovo,
the Becchi folk trudged the three miles morning and evening to hear the two sermons. In
the early hours of the night, the villagers all
tramped home together to their different ham-
lets. So it came about one evening that Don*
Calosso, the old parish priest of Murialdo, walk-
ing with the rest, became aware of a dark-eyed,
curly-headed urchin who seemed to him much
too young to be able to follow the instructions.

"Hello, Sonny," he said, "where are you from?"

"Becchi, Father."

"Could you understand anything of the sermon?"

"Yes, Father, all of it."

"All, that's a good deal. If you'll give me one
thought from it, I'll give you a penny."

"Which part, Father, the first or the second?"

"Whichever you like, even the subject of the
sermon."

---

*Don (Master), the title given to priests in Italy.

"It was on the necessity of not putting off one's conversion."

"And what did he say about it?"

"He put it in three parts, Father—which am I to say?"

"The one you like."

"Well, I'll say all three."

Whereupon this amazing urchin delivered the substance of the whole sermon. The villagers had gathered around the pair and, to the music of the child's clear voice, the way home seemed wonderfully short.

"That was one sermon," said the priest; "how about the other? Tell me something about that."

"What struck me most about it," said John gravely, "was this," and he recited vividly a scene dramatized by the preacher.

Don Calosso was dumbfounded. What a child! What intelligence and what a memory! What would the future bring? He paced, silent and thoughtful. "What is your name? Where do you live? Who are your parents? And where are you at school?" he asked at length.

"I am John Bosco, my father died when I was two, my mother has five of us to feed. I can read and write a little."

"Any knowledge of grammar?"

"What's that?"

"Would you like to study?"

"My brother Anthony won't have it."

"Why?"

"He says I know enough to work in the fields."

"Would you like to study?"

"Oh, yes."

"Why?"

"To be a priest."

"Why do you want to be a priest?"

"To get hold of the children, to teach them their religion, so that they may not grow up bad. I know that when they get bad, it's because they haven't had anyone to help them. Excuse me, Father, here is the turn to Becchi."

"Can you serve Mass, John?"

"A little."

"Then come and serve mine tomorrow."

Next day after Mass, there was a long conversation in which Don Calosso read the soul of the child and saw something of God's purpose for him. "Tell your mother to come and see me," he said on parting; "we will talk things over." In that talk it was decided that John should go to Murialdo every morning and study Latin with the old priest. The rest of the day he would go on working in the fields. Anthony was very angry when he heard what was afoot but for the moment held his peace.

Little John was radiantly happy with the kind, gentle, old priest—just the kind of priest he had dreamed of—not cold and distant like some he had met. He found Latin stiff, but went at it with all the vigor he possessed, and his wonderful memory was a great asset.

But the springtime came, and the few hours of study taken from field work roused Anthony's wrath. John did double work to make up and kept his books hidden till nightfall, but all was in vain. One night the elder brother broke out. "That's enough!" he raged. "I'm going to turn all these books out of the house. I became a big, strong man without any of that nonsense." John was hot too. "Our donkey's stronger still," said he, "and he never studied either." Anthony made a dash for him, but John fled through the open door.

Anthony's opposition soon became something like persecution. Margaret saw that this would not do. She stopped the lessons, but when this did not suffice she sent her beloved John away from home. "Go and get work on one of the farms round about," she said through her tears, and on a frosty morning in 1829 John Bosco, aged 14, with his small possessions tied up in a bundle, left home and committed himself to the Providence of God. He was hired as laborer to a fairly rich farmer of Moncucco. He worked hard all the week and on Sunday gathered the children of the hamlet together to teach them their religion, using his power of dramatic story-telling as a bribe.

But John's desire for the priesthood was more acute than ever; he confided it to his employers, who were very fond of him but gave him little encouragement. "It costs so much to be a priest, John."

"Cost what it may, I will go on hoping," he said, and spent all his evenings in study.

The year was not over when hope dawned. One day when shepherding the cattle he met his uncle Michael Occhiena, a well-to-do peasant, who had always liked him.

"Hello, John; getting on well?"

"Everyone is very kind to me, but I cannot get over the longing to carry on my studies. I shall soon be 15."

"Here," said his uncle, "take the cattle back to the farm, pack your bundle and go home."

It was not a triumphant homecoming. Margaret had to hide her son behind a hedge until Uncle Michael arrived to make and uphold the decision that John was to continue his education. Shortly afterwards the little family property was divided; Anthony set up on his own account, and Joseph was ready to do all he could for his younger brother. Margaret was free at last to devote her resources to her younger son. Even so there was little enough, had not Don

Calosso come again to the rescue. He adopted John for the time being and devoted himself entirely to his education, promising to provide for its continuance. John was supremely happy with the old man, whom he loved as a father, but his troubles were not at an end. Within the year the old priest died of a sudden stroke. His last look was for John. Taking the key of his cashbox from under his pillow, he gave it to him. But in the absence of any legal right, John handed it over to the nephew of the dead priest. "Take all that you need," said the latter; "I know that was my uncle's wish."

The temptation—for so John looked at it—was great, but he did what he thought was right. "I will take nothing," he said. But night was in his soul as he went back to Becchi.

Once again Uncle Michael played providence. He sent John to the school at Castelnuovo, where there was a supplementary class of Latin. It was a long way. To save shoe leather, John walked barefoot till he neared the little town, and as he thought the journeys to and fro a great waste of time, he did not go home at midday. And in bad weather he spent the night with a kindly tailor who gave him a hole under the staircase to sleep in. In the end the tailor offered to keep him altogether for a very small sum.

The big boy of 15 felt a little out of place

and awkward among the younger children. He was classed at first among the backward, but soon came to the top. The teacher had small sympathy for the big peasant lad, whose silent reserve made him appear stupid. "What can one expect from a place like Becchi?" he said. John was told that he was wasting his time at Latin and ought to go back to the plow. When his work was good, it was supposed that he had copied someone else. John made no answer; he accepted sarcasms silently and worked strenuously. Finally the Latin master declared that he would not read John's rubbish, and when John presented his translation, he threw it aside with a contemptuous remark about "dunces from Becchi." The class was amused; the others asked to hear John's nonsense, and the master, taking up his translation to please them, glanced through it. To his disgust it was almost faultless. "It is not his own," he said, "he has copied it from a neighbor."

"He has not," averred his two nearest neighbors; "read ours and see." The remark was only just, but it irritated the professor extremely.

"You think you can teach me," he retorted. "When I say he has copied, he has copied." It is not surprising that that kind of teaching was not very profitable to the pupils. John profited in another way, by the practice of patience and humility. More was to be learned from his friend the tailor; he could at least pick up something there, and indeed, he picked up a good deal. To begin with, he picked up tailoring and soon became so good at the work that he was almost able to pay for his board. He little knew how valuable this would be to him in later life. Moreover, Robert the tailor was something of a musician; he had a very fine voice and was first tenor in the choir. John, who had a beautiful voice himself, was a precious recruit. It did not take him long to learn the liturgical music, the hymns and canticles of the Church, and the learning was sheer joy. Most Italians are musical; he learned from Robert to play the violin. In a corner of the house was an elementary and rather decrepit harpsichord. John learned to play that too and practiced till he was an adept at accompaniments. This was the value he got out of his year at Castelnuovo in view of his future life—something that was to be even more precious to him than study.

When the summer holidays came around, John went back to his work in the fields. What was going to happen now? The answer was another dream.

There came to him in this dream a shepherdess, beautiful beyond compare, leading a large flock of sheep. "John," she called, "come here. Do you see this flock of mine? Look, I give it into your keeping."

"My Lady," said John, "what can I do? How can I keep this great flock of sheep and lambs? I have no pasture for them."

"Don't be afraid," said she. "I will watch over you, and I will help you."

The next day he met a friendly farmer. "John, what makes you look so jolly today?" he asked. "You've looked rather grave and worried of late."

"Today," said John triumphantly, "I know with certainty that I shall be a priest."

Chapter 2

THE MENDING
OF A BROKEN HOPE

THE YEAR at Castelnuovo having proved more or less a failure insofar as John's studies were concerned, his mother made a bold resolve. He should go to the school at Chieri. But this was going to be expensive. Margaret gave all that she could spare—some 50 pounds of corn and six bushels of millet, friendly neighbors gladly contributed the little they could, while a friend undertook to convey John's modest fortune into Chieri in his cart. John, now a tall boy of 16, tramped with his mother to Castelnuovo carrying on his shoulders two sacks of grain, which they sold in the marketplace to buy books and writing materials. Then they went on to Chieri.

The grain had already been delivered at the door of the little house of Lucia Matta, a widow, where John was to lodge. "Here is the payment for his room and his board," said Margaret. "I have done all that I can. Providence will do the rest." To eke out the money for his board, it had been agreed that John should act as servant to the widow and help a little boy of nine with his lessons. Margaret went home with a glad heart. At last that beloved youngest son of hers was definitely on his way to the priesthood. One day she would receive her Lord from his hand; one day she would bow her head for his blessing.

For John the beginnings were not too easy. He knew a good deal, but since his studies had been very disjointed, he was placed in the sixth class among the little children. The master was kind to him, however, and gave him private tutoring. John worked hard, as he always did, and in two months was sent up to the fifth class. In two months more he was in the fourth, but even here his size was remarkable. The master was a strict disciplinarian. "This big fellow must be either a great fool or a bit of a genius," he remarked. John laughed. "Something between the two," he said; "just a boy who wants to work hard and do his duty."

The master liked the ready answer. "If you want work, you will get it," he said, "and if you work well, you can count on me to help you."

The boys took to John, and a circumstance that happened later made him still more of a favorite. One morning he forgot his *Cornelius*

Nepos, the Latin book on which they were at
work and, to evade notice, held his Latin grammar open before him while he listened atten-
tively to the reading and explanations of pupils
and master. Some of his nearest companions
began to laugh. Soon others joined in, and the
angry master, seeing all eyes fixed on John, bade
him get up and repeat the lesson. With scarcely
a hesitation, John repeated both passage and
explanations, whereupon the class burst into noisy
applause. This still further increased the master's
wrath. He had never been confronted with such
indiscipline before. A boy explained. "Bosco is
constructing *Cornelius* out of his Latin grammar." The master, who could hardly believe his
ears, ended by joining in the applause. "God
has given you a wonderful gift," he said; "make
good use of it."

The power of John's influence soon asserted
itself, although in his early days at Chieri—like
every boy in a crowd of companions of all kinds—
he had to take a definite stand against evil. There
were invitations to join a gaming group, pro-
posals to rob fields and gardens, and one young
hopeful even suggested that he steal his land-
lady's watch and buy candy with the proceeds.

John avoided this type of boy, but there was
nothing sanctimonious about him. He banded
his friends into a group which he called the

Merry Company, and merry they were, though it was significant of John's methods that all the members had solemnly to pledge themselves to say or do nothing unworthy of a Christian. On Sundays and feast days after Mass, he would lead his little troop out into the hills, singing as they went, with a meal of bread and chestnuts in their pockets, to come back tired and happy at nightfall. He had not forgotten his acrobatic tricks, and his story-telling powers were as vivid as ever. He sometimes sang and sometimes played the violin. He was a good entertainer, and his motto was what it was to the end of his life: Enjoy yourself as much as you like, if only you keep from sin. The society prospered and grew, and John was the soul of it. Every member was encouraged to use what talents he had for the benefit of the rest, to be always cheerful, and above all to put God's interests first. It was understood that to be "merry" meant to take things as they came and to make the best of them; John knew something about that.

After two years, John's little pupil no longer required his services. John had to look for other lodgings, which he found in the shop of a pastry cook who ran a small restaurant as well. Every day before he went to school, John had to clean up the shop, and when he came back at evening there was more work to be done. In return for this, he had a little dark alcove under the stairs, where, by the light of a tallow candle, he studied far into the night. Every Saturday his mother brought him a loaf and what she could spare in the way of chestnuts or vegetables, but he was often desperately hungry. One young comrade, the son of a prosperous farmer who had an apple orchard, noticed this, and would sometimes slip his own apples into John's pocket, a kindness which the latter never forgot.

A favorite Sunday excursion of the Merry Company was to Turin, where, after visiting the famous chapel of the Holy Shroud and the historical monuments of the town, they would end up in the afternoon at the chapel of the Jesuit Fathers to hear the weekly instruction on Christian doctrine. One Sunday, an acrobat elected to set up his stall in the neighboring square and was preparing a choice performance to take place at the very hour of the sermon. The weaker members hesitated—popular as the instructions were, the acrobat was irresistible. John made a rapid decision. He breathed a prayer and challenged the acrobat to a trial of skill. The man was not averse to the proposal—it might bring him more spectators. "First, a race," he declared, "and 20 dollars to the winner." John had no money, but his friends contributed on the spot.

The race was run and won—by John. The professional was piqued but not discouraged. "The long jump!" he cried: "40 dollars."

"All right," said John, "40 dollars." A spot was chosen where the river was not only fairly wide, but bounded on the opposite side by a low wall. A very nasty jump. The acrobat did it beautifully, alighting neatly on the little strip of earth below the wall.

"Not easy to do much better than that," and the man smiled satirically as John poised for his jump. But not for long. With one flying leap John was over the river—and the wall. It was a crushing defeat, but his angry rival was determined to beat him yet. "Choose whatever you like, and I'll beat you at it," he said.

"The magic stick," said John, taking the offensive: "80 dollars." He set his hat on the top of a stick, balanced it on the palm of his hand, on each finger, on his elbow, his shoulder, chin, mouth, nose and head, and brought it triumphantly back by the same road.

"Give it here," said the man, "I'll show you." He did it beautifully. The stick seemed to be dancing, but his nose was rather long. On the return journey the stick, coming in contact with the tip, lost its equilibrium, and the man had to put up a hand to steady it. David had beaten Goliath for the third time, and Goliath was furious. "A hundred dollars," he cried, "to the one who touches the highest point of that elm tree!"

"Very well," said John, elated with his success, "100 dollars." Throwing off coat and waistcoat, the man climbed rapidly up the tree till he reached a branch that bent under his weight. It was impossible to go higher. Amid the loud applause of the bystanders he came down. "Poor old John, you've lost this time," whispered a friend.

"That remains to be seen," said John. He made the Sign of the Cross and began to climb. Swiftly he went up and up till he reached the branch where his rival had stopped. Then, to the breathless astonishment of all, he grasped the bough with both hands, and, with a sudden swing of his supple young body, reversed his position and balanced himself thus for a moment, his feet above the topmost branch. The applause was delirious. John had won all down the line; an angry and resentful rival was before him. The Merry Company did not like that, so they invited the acrobat to a modest meal at the neighboring inn and let him off with the payment of the bill—and the promise that he would not come there again at that hour.

There were in John's class, at the school in Chieri, several Jews who were in difficulties about their Saturday's work. For them it was the Sabbath, when all work was forbidden. But the older boys used to laugh at them as if it were a pretext for getting an extra vacation day. John, who saw that it was a question of conscience, used to send them a list of the work given out, with the explanations. In consequence, they vowed him an eternal friendship, and one of them, who used to frequent the restaurant where John worked, became very intimate with him. One day this young fellow, whose name was Jonas, got mixed up in a school scrape and, anxious about the consequences, came to consult his friend.

"If you were a Christian," said John, "I should take you straight off to Confession, but that can't be done."

"Why not? We can go to Confession if we like."

"Perhaps, but you have no Sacrament of Penance, no power to forgive sins, no guarantee of secrecy."

"I will go to a Catholic priest if you like."

"You can't unless you are baptized and believe in Jesus Christ."

"What would they say at home?"

"If God calls you to this, He will protect you."

"What would you do if you were in my place?" asked the young Jew.

"I would begin to study the catechism," said John.

The advice was taken; John prayed. Light and conviction came to Jonas, but the catechism was discovered. Irate parents took it to the Rabbi and accused John of betraying the friendship and ruining the soul of their son. Both friends had a good deal to suffer; there were even threats of violence. Jonas had to leave home, but he stood firm in his determination to become a Catholic. In the end, friends came to his assistance, the young Jew was baptized and the tumult died down. Several others followed him into the Church.

John, as we have seen, was an accomplished "magician" or illusionist. Mischievously, he would sometimes try his tricks on his host, who began at last to suspect the cooperation of the devil. This man had gathered from his rather superficial knowledge of the catechism that men could not do such things, and certainly God would not waste His time on such foolishness. He took the matter to his parish priest. "Father, I am afraid I am sheltering a young man who has dealings with the devil," he said, and began recounting a long history of weird occurrences. The priest referred the case to the archpriest of the cathedral, a venerable old canon who ordered John to come up for examination. He was accordingly put through the catechism—he had it at his fingertips. He was questioned as to his life and his associates. He answered frankly—not a trace of deceit or malice.

"My young friend," said the canon gravely, "I hear strange things about you. I am told you can read the thoughts of others, know what is happening at a distance, and can make white black and black white. Who has taught you all this?"

"Reverend Father," said John quietly, "will you give me five minutes to answer you? What is the time?"

The canon felt for his watch—it was not there.

"Could you give me a quarter?" asked John.

The canon put his hand in his pocket—it was empty.

"You rascal!" he cried, "you have taken my watch and my purse!"

"Reverend Father," said John, "it only needs a little quickness and a little skill to do this kind of thing. It is simple enough. When I came in you had just given an alms to a beggar whom I met at the door, and you left your purse on the kneeler. In passing into your study, you left your watch on the table in the corridor. I picked them both up as I came in, and here they are under the lampshade." The examination ended in a burst of laughter.

In most vocations to the priesthood, there comes a moment of doubt and hesitation—a sense of unworthiness, a moment which the tempter often uses to suggest that such a high calling is beyond the strength of mortal man, that human nature is weak, and that a good life in the world is safer and more wholesome. It came to John as to others. The memory of his dreams had grown dim, the knowledge of his weakness made him afraid. A sense of his unworthiness abashed him. He went to his confessor for advice, but his confessor would not face the responsibility of deciding. "In the matter of vocation," he said, "everyone must follow his own inclinations." What were his inclinations, John asked himself. Was he to be a Franciscan like the friars he revered so much, or a Dominican like his masters at the school? Would not life be quieter and safer in a religious order than in the secular priesthood? He determined to consult his mother—that wise adviser who had always left him free in his choice of life. The holidays were approaching, and with them his opportunity.

"The only thing I want of you," she said, "is the salvation of your soul. Follow God's will."

After much prayer, John decided in favor of the Franciscans, and had resolved to enter there when he was advised to consult Don Cafasso (St. Joseph Cafasso), a saintly young priest who had the gift of guiding souls. There was no hesitation in his reply: John was for the secular priesthood. "Go on studying," he said, "then to the seminary, and there hold yourself in readiness to follow the guidance of God."

For John it was decisive. He went back to Chieri to his studies and worked harder than ever. He was the most popular boy in the school, first in his class, an athlete, a musician, everybody's friend, always ready to do a good turn to anyone—a potent influence for good.

Fifteen months later, in October 1835, in the church of Castelnuovo where he had been baptized 20 years before, he received from the hands of his parish priest the cassock of the clerical student, and five days later said good-bye to his mother. The day before his departure to the seminary, when the little party of friends and relations who had helped to provide his outfit had all gone, Margaret Bosco laid her hands upon his shoulders. "My little John," she said, looking up at the tall young son who was so much bigger than she, "to see you with the cassock fills my heart with joy. But remember that it is not the habit that gives honor to the state, but the practice of virtue. If at any time you should come to doubt of your vocation, I beseech you to lay it aside at once; I would rather have a poor peasant for my son than a negligent priest. When you came into the world, I consecrated you to Our Lady; when you began to study, I bade you honor her and have recourse to her in all your difficulties; now I beg you to take her for your Queen." The two clung together, deeply moved.

"Mother," said John after a long silence, "before I leave you to take up this new life, let me thank you for all you have done for me. Your teaching will live always in my soul, a treasure that has made me rich forever."

John Bosco had obtained the goal of his hopes, a goal which had seemed so impossible. Don Guala, Rector of the Ecclesiastical College at Turin, had offered to pay for his first year at the seminary. For the two following years, he won the prize of 60 dollars, given for the highest place in studies and good conduct. In his second year of philosophy, he gained the sum granted to needy and promising students; the money always came—somehow. Perhaps Margaret's prayers had something to do with it.

John loved his teachers, but found them very distant. It was the custom to visit the superiors on arriving and departing. At other times, unless summoned for a reproof, there was no chance to talk. John often longed to ask advice or to talk over a difficulty. He resolved that when he came to the priesthood, he would always have an open door for boys and young men and make himself their friend and companion.

His six years at the seminary were fruitful in every way. A great worker and very intelligent, he got through the day's work with a speed that left him a good deal of leisure time, which he employed in studying foreign languages and the history of the Church. As always, he was a good comrade, never tired of helping others. The devout faith and the intense love of God that was in him had nothing morose about it; he was the liveliest and the gayest of companions. His goodness was a most attractive thing—and catching. He was never known to grumble and was never cross. To him the daily trials of life were something that might be offered to God. Easy? No. These things have to be fought for and won at the sword's point—the race is to the swift and the victory to the strong. There were many sore battles, as there must always be for those who have high ideals.

During one summer vacation, when the cholera had caused the Jesuit College in Turin to break up earlier than usual, John was asked to direct the Greek studies of some of their older pupils. They were well-read, intelligent young men, sons of well-to-do fathers, but John was quickly convinced that his apostolate did not lie in that direction. He contrasted them with his boisterous, often dirty little friends of Becchi, Castelnuovo and Chieri, who, always faithful to him, invaded the seminary parlors on Sundays and holidays, chattering, laughing and quite ready to be led off to the chapel for prayer. When, in solemn file, the seminarians went to High Mass at the cathedral, they would lie in wait, watching for him. "Do you see that young cleric, the one with curly hair? Well, that's our friend, you've no idea how good he is!" Their friend, yes—partly because they were friendless and partly because he knew he was meant for them.

Toward the end of his years as a seminarian, one night during vacation, another vivid dream came to confirm the message of the others. Below his brother's farm where he was staying was a wide valley which suddenly became a great city. Everywhere in the streets and the squares were boys, young ruffians, wholly uncared for, howling, cursing and fighting. John, as before, dashed in among them to make them stop—he could never bear the sound of blasphemy—but they hit back vigorously and he was obliged to retreat. Again he was met by the mysterious Stranger. "Go back," He said, "and try persuasion; here is My Mother, let her guide you." It was the lovely Shepherdess that he had seen before, and she was looking at him with kindly eyes.

"If you really want to win these little outcasts," she said, "you will do it only by gentleness and kindness." Christ and His Blessed

Mother, bending in loving pity over the moral misery of their children, had chosen John Bosco to be their shepherd and, once more, in a dream, had pointed out the way.

As a theological student, John had distinguished himself; he had the gift of expressing himself with clearness and eloquence and had preached his first sermon two years before he was ordained. That he had a gift for extemporizing was proved by an incident that occurred a year later at Cinzano, when the preacher who had been invited to preach on the feast of St. Roch failed to appear. In his sympathy for the parish priest, John tried to induce some of the priests who were present to come to the rescue. "You seem to think it's quite an easy thing to improvise a sermon on St. Roch," they retorted. "If it's as simple a thing as that, why don't you do it yourself instead of bothering others?" "I wouldn't have dared to offer," replied John, "but if no one else will, I'll try."

In after years he used to say that he had never preached so well. Yet he was wise enough to realize that a too ready gift might be a snare, and he consulted a priest friend whom he trusted. "Your sermon was beautiful," was the reply, "well worked out, quotations appropriate and diction excellent. Go on like that and you will be a successful preacher."

"Successful?" asked John dubiously; "did the people understand?"

"Very little. What seems simple enough to you is often above their heads."

"What am I to do?"

"This. Drop the literary style, speak—as far as possible—the language of the people, and speak with great simplicity. Don't be too long; keep to the point. Remember that the people know far too little of the truths of the Faith and that you can never explain them too clearly."

"That advice has lasted me for my whole life," said John in later years. "I saw at once the pretentiousness of my early preaching and the vain glory that was behind it."

At the Seminary of Chieri, it was the custom to write a few words opposite the name of each student. Opposite John Bosco's was the verdict: "Full of zeal and most promising." It was the opinion of all. "That fellow will do something great," said one who had lived for five years in close contact with him.

In 1840, at Turin, John received Minor Orders, in the Lent of 1841 he received the diaconate, and in May of the same year he began his retreat for the priesthood. A few of the thoughts and resolutions that came to him during that time of prayer and preparation may well be noted. They were written in a shabby little notebook that he kept to the end of his life.

"No priest goes either to Heaven or to Hell alone; faithful or unfaithful, he carries many with him. When it is a question of the salvation of souls, I will always be prepared to humble myself, to suffer and to act." "I will try to carry everywhere with me the sweetness and gentleness of my patron, St. Francis of Sales." "Since work is such a power against the enemies of the soul, I will not allow myself more than five hours' sleep."

On the day after his ordination, John said his first Mass in the Church of St. Francis of Assisi. He had asked that it might be very quiet, very simple, that he might pour out his soul in thanksgiving to God, who had thus crowned the hope of his childhood. And all through the Mass he was haunted by the thought of the unknown flock of his dream, waiting for him, somewhere, in God's future. And at the solemn moment of the Elevation, he asked God to give him the grace of winning souls.

On the following Thursday, the Feast of Corpus Christi, he yielded to the desire of all his kinfolk and friends and sang the High Mass at Castelnuovo. Afterwards, there was a great festival at the presbytery, to which relations, benefactors and all the clergy of the neighboring parishes were invited. Congratulations were hearty and vivacious, but the new priest was glad when it was all over and he was left alone with his mother. They walked home together in the twilight to Becchi, and every yard of the way was full of memories. So many dreams, so many hopes—broken hopes, so often—and now, the glorious realization. And through them all, the strong and tender hand of a woman, leading, guiding him through difficulties, through seeming impossibilities—the loving hand of the mother who walked at his side, her heart too full for words.

And now they were at home again—the little home of his childhood. His mother lit the candle, set things in order for the night, and they knelt together as of old for the evening prayer. And when they rose, Margaret, who had been very silent all day, took the two hands of her son in her own.

"My John," she said, "you are now a priest, and every day you will have the joy of saying Mass. But remember this: to say Mass is to unite yourself with the Crucified—to begin to suffer. You will not notice it at first, but in time you will see that I was right. Every day, I know, you will pray for me; that is all I ask. Think of nothing but the salvation of souls."

Chapter 3

THE TEMPERING OF THE STEEL

DON BOSCO was soon to make closer acquaintance with the city of his dream, in whose streets homeless and vagrant boys found a fruitful school of vice. The parish of Murialdo was vacant and asking for him; the archpriest of Castelnuovo, his old friend, was begging for him as curate. Once more he consulted the saintly Don Cafasso, Rector of the Ecclesiastical Institute in Turin. "Come back," was the answer, "and complete your priestly formation with us."

The Institute had been founded for the training of young priests in parish work. They attended lectures in Moral Theology and, under the guidance of Don Cafasso, visited the prisons and poorer quarters of the city. The sight of boys of 12 and 13 undergoing sentences for small breaches of the law, in the horrible surrounding of prison life as it was at that time, filled John Bosco with horror. "Once in," he was told, "they seldom remain long out." Conviction after conviction followed, till a life of evil too often closed with a dreadful death.

"Can nothing be done," he asked himself, "to save these young lives from ruin? If these forsaken young creatures had had someone to care for them, would they be where they are?" In the anguish of his soul he went to Don Cafasso, and they tried to think out some scheme of action.

The quiet old city of Turin had been suddenly industrialized, with the usual results. Behind its stately buildings there were districts where it was hardly safe to go, where vice and crime reigned untrammelled. When John went out into these neighborhoods, he found many boys and young men who had come in from the country and, unable to find work, had taken to loafing about the streets. From the factories and workshops, in the evening, there would pour out a crowd of young people, many of them mere boys, cursing, swearing and fighting. Here was his dream come true, but what could he do?

He was vesting for Mass on the Feast of the Immaculate Conception in the sacristy of the Church of St. Francis of Assisi when, at the sound of an angry voice, he turned to see the sacristan beating a big boy with the stick with which he had been lighting the candles.

"What has he done?" asked the young priest. "Let him alone."

"He says he can't serve Mass—then what is he doing in the sacristy?" was the answer.

"No harm at all," said John. "I won't have my friends treated like that."

"Your friend!" said the sacristan. "That rascal!"

"The very fact that he's in trouble makes him my friend," said John. "Get him back"—for the boy had fled.

The sacristan, rather abashed, went out and came back with the lad, terrified at what might be going to happen to him.

"What is your name, my boy?"

"Bartholomew Garelli."

"Are you working?"

"Yes, as a mason."

"Is your father alive?"

"No."

"Your mother?"

"Dead, too."

"How old are you?"

"Sixteen."

"Can you read or write?"

"No."

"Sing or whistle?"

The boy laughed, and the ice was broken.

"Tell me, son, have you made your First Communion?"

"No."

"Have you ever been to Confession?"

"Long ago, when I was little."

"Do you say any prayers?"

"I have forgotten them."

"Do you go to Mass on Sundays?"

"Yes, I generally do that."

"Do you go to catechism class?"

"I don't dare. Because I am so big, the little boys would know more than me."

"If I taught you, would you come?"

"Of course!"

"When shall we begin? Today?"

"If you like."

"Look here, I am going to say Mass now. You stay for it, and afterwards we will set to work."

In a little room behind the sacristy the first lesson was given—the first step on the road that was to lead so far. The priest knelt and put his whole heart into a Hail Mary, that this young soul might be won for God.

"Can you make the Sign of the Cross, Bartholomew?"

The boy stared. That first lesson of the Catholic child was unknown to him.

"Will you come back, Bartholomew?"

"That I will."

"Bring others with you, then—your friends."

Bartholomew did. Next Sunday he brought six and Don Cafasso picked up two more. In a few months there were 80, mostly apprentices, and good fellows at heart, though utterly ignorant. The friendly interest of their young patron, the charm of his talk, his wonderful way with boys, won their trust completely; they haunted him at every free moment. And he had only his little room in which to receive them, no money but his small Mass fee. What was to be done?

Don Cafasso, enchanted at the growing apostolate and realizing its significance, gave up to John the yard of the Institute. It was an unselfish gift, for the windows of the house looked out on it, and with a hundred or so young hooligans yelling and romping in a not over large space, it was goodbye to the quiet Sunday rest. But what did it matter if souls were being won for God?

For three years the "Oratory," as they called it, was held there until Don Bosco's time at the Institute was up. Don Cafasso, who realized the worth of his young friend's apostolate and who feared above all things that he might be whisked off to a country parish, succeeded in obtaining for him the chaplaincy of an orphanage—the Refuge of St. Philomena at Valdocco, a suburb of Turin, founded by the Marchioness Barolo. This great lady, very rich and very charitable, but also very autocratic, was a widow who devoted herself almost entirely to works of benevolence.

Her orphanage, or Refuge, as she preferred to call it, was for girls, and John was to be curate to Don Borel, the head chaplain. Don Borel, who was full of sympathy for John's work among his boys, induced the Marchioness to allow them to come to him at the Refuge.

On the first Sunday of Don Bosco's residence there, the inhabitants of Valdocco were more than a little startled at the sight of a crowd of noisy young ruffians demanding to know where Don Bosco had his quarters and where they would find the new Oratory. There was an indignant protest which threatened to end in violence, when Don Bosco suddenly appeared and restored all to order. Who was this young man, they asked each other, who seemed to be the friend of every young rascal in Turin? They talked it over to such purpose that they ended in asking that their own boys should join the company. John was ready for them all, and by All Saints Day there were more than 200 for Confession. Don Borel lent his ready help—he was to become one of Don Bosco's most enthusiastic champions—and the boys waited their turn patiently. Two big rooms at the Refuge had been arranged as a chapel, and a long, wide corridor served as playroom.

On Sundays and feast days, most of the boys came to Mass, and some of the older ones were beginning to help with the new arrivals. Don Bosco even started some evening classes where the two priests, using their own rooms as class-rooms, taught the first elements of education.

Such a state of things was too good to last long however. Letters began to rain upon the Marchioness. The boys were unbearably noisy, their presence so near the Refuge was undesir-able, and—most serious of all—they had picked flowers out of the garden! The outcome was an invitation to Don Bosco to take his obnoxious family elsewhere. *"Dio Mio*, what shall I do with these lambs of mine?" he wondered as he explored the neighboring district in search of new quarters.

One day, he came to the cemetery of St. Peter in Chains. It had a big chapel behind it that was used solely for funerals, and beyond lay a large piece of waste ground overgrown with this-tles. "Just the thing," he thought, and the chap-lain proved to be a kind old priest who was quite ready to let him have the use of the chapel and the field on Sundays. The boys were dis-tressed at first to hear that the Oratory was to be moved, but Don Bosco cheered them up by explaining that if you want young cabbages to grow, they must be frequently transplanted; and when, on the following Sunday, they came to their new quarters, they were delighted. They ran and jumped and shouted with joy in the open space, which was so much easier to play in than the close corridor at the Refuge.

The old chaplain was away, but alas, his house-keeper was at home. The door of the rectory suddenly burst open and she emerged, the very frill of her cap bristling with fury. "Is it you," she cried, shaking an angry fist at Don Bosco, "who are the leader of this gang of ruffians? It's the last time you'll meet here, profaning holy places!"

"Stop playing, boys," said Don Bosco, "we will go to the chapel for catechism and Rosary." Later on in the afternoon, the boys played again in the open space, Don Bosco rejoicing to see them romping as healthy young creatures have a right to romp, and in the evening they went home enchanted with their day in the open air.

But the chaplain came home too in the evening, and—well—Holy Writ has something to say on the disadvantages of a brawling woman in the house. Don Bosco was requested to come there no more.

"Courage," he said to his little flock, "moving seems to suit us; we are growing all the time. God is our Father and He will take care of us."

A few weeks later he discovered a little church dedicated to St. Martin near some flour mills. Mass was said there on Sunday, after which it was empty for the rest of the day. He could use it for catechism. True, at Mass it was so full that his boys could hardly get in at all, and for recreation there was only the little square in front of it or the adjoining streets, fairly full of traffic; still, it was better than nothing. The people who worked at the mills, however, did not appreciate the noisy invasion of their district. They wrote a long letter of complaint to the town council, representing the boys in the worst possible light. Don Bosco was refused the use of the church; he was to leave at once.

It was mid-winter. His invincible courage now conceived what might be termed a "pilgrim Oratory." In the early morning, the boys assembled very quietly at Don Bosco's house. Those who could brought some provisions in their pockets and shared with those who could not. Still quietly, with Don Bosco at their head, they proceeded to some church in the neighboring country where they heard Mass. Then, after breakfast in the open air and a short instruction, there were games and recreation, then they went on to another sanctuary for Vespers. Catechism and Rosary followed, and then a long walk back to the town in the quiet of the evening. This was delightful in fine weather, but not so admirable in wet. Don Bosco decided that such a state of things could not last long. He rented two rooms in the city—small enough accommodation for the crowd he had, but the evening classes could go on, and they could go out when the weather was fine. But this too was only to last for a few months. Fresh complaints about noise and rumors that Don Bosco was a revolutionary, training a young army for purposes of mischief ended in another request to go elsewhere.

Again the Oratory was homeless, and Don Bosco once more began his search. He ended by renting a large field near the public road. There the group met on Sundays in the early morning, when Don Bosco, sitting on a little mound, heard Confessions while the rest played at a little distance. Then, called together by an old drum beaten by one of the boys, they set off quietly for the church where they were to hear Mass, after which they came back to their field and the open-air pulpit of their master. Unfriendly and mischievous comments now became so rife that policemen were told to prowl around the field and find out what was going on in the way of revolutionary propaganda. Don Bosco, quite aware of their neighborhood and ready to make full use of the opportunity, adapted his instructions to the needs of their souls.

"Strange kind of a revolutionary, that," they said, "we'll be going to Confession if we go there much longer. If all the boys in Turin were as

well behaved as these, there would be no need
of policemen."

Even many of Don Bosco's best friends thought
it was a crazy undertaking. "You see that circumstances are against you," they said. "Cut
down your numbers, take only a few of the worst
cases." And when they failed to convince him,
they looked at each other and touched their fore-
heads. "It's a monomania," they said, "and it's
growing." They told him he was an idealist.

"Not at all," he said, "I see things plainly as
they are. Soon we shall have churches, vast play-
grounds, priests, helpers of all kinds and thousands of boys."

"Poor Don Bosco," they said, shaking their
heads, "such a good young priest, what a pity!
We really ought to do something."

One day, two clerics of Turin, one a reverend
canon, came to visit him in his little room at
the Refuge. "Come for a drive," they said, "we
have a carriage at the door. It will do you good."

"Delighted," said Don Bosco; "wait till I get
my hat."

He escorted them downstairs, opened the door
of the carriage and bowed.

"You get in first," they said.

"I could not think of it," said Don Bosco
politely.

They insisted—so did he; they had to yield.

No sooner were they in than he closed the door sharply.

"To the lunatic asylum quick," he called to the coachman, who had had his orders and set off at a gallop.

"My goodness!" said the attendants who were waiting at the door. "Two of them, and both violent!" It was only with the greatest difficulty that the head doctor was persuaded of their sanity. Don Bosco was no longer mentioned.

His endurance, however, was once more tested. The owners of the field declared that the tramping of the boys had completely destroyed their grass. "We will give you two weeks to get out," they said. Two weeks!

At the end of a week, no place could be found! At the end of the second, still nothing. Must the work be given up? It was his last day. The boys met as usual, merry and joyous, but Don Bosco's heart was like lead. "Off now," he ordered, "to Our Lady of the Fields. We will ask a great grace of her. We will pray together." With the intuition of love, they guessed there was something wrong and prayed with all their hearts. Then they went back to their field, and games began as usual. Don Bosco paced up and down, blind with tears; for once his spirit was broken. "O my God," he prayed, "help me, show me what to do."

As he prayed, a man came onto the field to meet him. "Is it true that you are looking for premises?" he said. "I have a friend called Pinardi who has a splendid shed to rent. Would you care to see it?"

Don Bosco followed him. The splendid shed was a large tumble-down structure with a very low roof. His hopes fell.

"We could dig out the floor a foot or two," said the man, "and board it. You could have the use of the surrounding land too, and all for 300 dollars a year."

"When?" asked Don Bosco.

"By next Sunday," said the man.

Don Bosco went back to his boys. At the news that henceforward they were to have a permanent abode, the poor little urchins went mad with joy. Singing and shouting they danced around him—that friend of the friendless, their own Don Bosco, till at last he bade them be quiet and say with him a Rosary of thanksgiving.

One anxiety ended, another arose. He was sent for by the Marchioness.

"I have decided," she said, "that you cannot do justice to my orphans when you have 400 boys to look after. The work is too hard for you. I think your heart is with the boys, and my affairs will suffer. You must give up either one or the other. Take a few days to think it over."

"I can answer you at once," was the answer. "You will find a dozen men to take my place at the Refuge. But if I give up my poor children, who will take my place there?"

"But where will you go? How will you live?"

"Providence will see to that."

"But you are worn out, you look wretched. Do be sensible. Go and take a long vacation— I will pay all the expenses, and then come back here and take up your work at the Refuge again."

"I am very grateful, but it is impossible. I have vowed to devote my life to these poor little outcasts. It is God's will—the path He has traced out for me."

The lady stiffened. "You prefer your little vagabonds to my orphans? Very well. You are at liberty to devote yourself entirely to them."

"I hope you are not going to turn me out like that," said Don Bosco gravely. "People would talk, and my priestly reputation would suffer."

"Very well, I give you three months' notice," said the indignant Marchioness. It was now John who was homeless.

The lady was right. He was worn out; the labor and anxiety of the last 20 months had done their work. One day, after an exhausting Sunday with his boys, he came home and fainted. In a few days, he was in a raging fever with

pneumonia and had received the last Sacraments.
His mother and brother had come to what they
believed to be his deathbed. His faithful friend
Don Borel hardly ever left him. His boys, hearing the terrible news, rushed with breaking hearts
to the house. Some of the older ones installed
themselves as nurses, replacing each other night
and day at regular intervals; others watched at
the door, on the stairs, in the street, on the mere
chance of being let in one moment to see their
beloved friend. Their pleas were pitiful. "Just let
me in one minute, I won't speak to him." "I
know he'd let me in if he knew I was here."
"Just open the door a tiny chink and let us have
one look at him." But the doctor's orders had
to be obeyed, and the boys had to be content
with a daily report.

Could it be possible that God was going to
abandon them—to take away their friend? If a
miracle was needed, they would get it; they
would pray so that they must be heard. Hour
by hour they went on in one unending Rosary.
They began early in the morning, praying on
till late into the night—some went on till dawn.
Big boys who all day long went up and down
ladders with hods of mortar on their backs, fasted
on bread and water. How completely Don Bosco
had won their hearts by his loving care—this
humble young priest who lay preparing his soul

for death. He was very near the end when Don Borel leaned over him.

"Pray that God may cure you," he said.

"May His holy Will be done," came the faint answer.

"Pray then, at least, that if it *is* His holy Will, He may cure you. Say it after me." Don Bosco obeyed.

"Now I know you will get well," said Don Borel happily. "Your own prayer was the only thing that was needed."

The next day, the doctor said there was hope. A few days later, Don Bosco was out of danger. In two weeks' time the door opened, and, pale and thin, he stood before the ecstatic eyes of his boys. An armchair had been provided. The bigger ones lifted it onto their shoulders, and shouting, singing and weeping with joy, they carried Don Bosco in solemn procession to the poor shed-chapel that was their very own. Two days later, he went home to Becchi to convalesce. The work of the Oratory, meanwhile, was kept going by friends, under the guidance of Don Borel.

They did not take long to realize what unwearying patience and devotedness was required to live in constant contact with this affectionate, but noisy, dirty, rough, ill-mannered and often verminous population: to go from factory to factory begging work for those who had none, to go on doggedly begging for help from any who could be induced to give it, to be full of affection and sympathy for the least attractive, the most unpromising of the crowd—in a word, to be a second John Bosco. But they stuck to it— for three months—while Don Bosco was gaining health and strength under his mother's care, and they saved the situation.

By this time, in spite of doctors, friends and acquaintances, he had come back to work. In Pinardi's house, close to the quasi-chapel, he rented two rooms for himself. But Pinardi's house, and the lodging house and tavern beside it, had not the best of reputations; it was not the ideal quarters for a priest. "Take your mother with you," said his friend, the good old dean of Castelnuovo. But his mother was no longer young. Could he ask her to exchange the peace of the little home at Becchi to live in the midst of four hundred noisy, ragged boys? He made a tentative suggestion.

"If you think it is God's will," she answered promptly, "take me." Knowing that it was abject poverty to which she was going, she made the sacrifice of her dearest treasures, selling even her wedding dress—stored away in lavender; it would bring in a little money.

On a November morning they set off together:

she with a little basket containing some linen
and household implements, he with his books
and breviary, tramping to Turin on foot, a seven
hours' walk. As they neared the city, dusty and
weary, they met a priest friend, Don Vola.

"Where do you come from?"

"Becchi."

"On foot?"

"Why, yes."

"Where are you going?"

"My mother is coming to live with me at
Pinardi's."

"What are you going to live on now that you
have lost your chaplaincy?"

"I don't know, but we trust in God, and He
will see us through."

"Are they expecting you at Pinardi's?"

Don Bosco laughed. "Not likely."

"How about your supper?"

"It doesn't matter, we'll see to it presently."

"My dear Don Bosco," said the priest with
tears in his eyes, "I wish I could do something
to help." He felt in his pocket—not a cent.

"Take this at least," he said, pulling out his
watch, and thrusting it into Don Bosco's hand,
the good priest fled.

A few more moments and they were at home—
two little rooms on the first floor, miserably furnished. Night had fallen. By the light of a single

candle, Margaret prepared a frugal supper while her son hung up a holy water font, a picture of Our Lady and a blessed palm. Under the windows, some of the boys had gathered, watching the flickering light and wondering if he had at last come back. Fearful lest it might be a stranger, they did not dare to investigate, when the silence was suddenly broken by a clear tenor voice and the weaker treble of a woman singing an evening hymn.

When Margaret woke up the next morning and looked at her surroundings, her heart may have been a little heavy. But not for long. She turned to John with a smile. "At Becchi," she said, "I had to be always at work, cleaning and setting things to rights and telling people what to do; but here I think I shall have a much easier time."

These were days of great anxiety for John. There was no money for the rent; the most wretched of the boys were always wanting food and clothing; many came to the door to beg for bread, and Margaret had not the heart to send them away. But it was not in vain that Don Bosco and his mother had put their trust in Providence. By the sale of a little land which belonged to them at Becchi and with other help, it soon became possible to rent three more rooms in Pinardi's house; these were used for night classes.

Don Bosco now began to form the earliest of his protégés to help him by teaching the younger ones. The reading book was the catechism; in that way it was possible to kill two birds with one stone. Soon there were arithmetic classes, classes for geography, drawing and singing. The elders Don Bosco taught himself. They came to him eagerly at every free moment and worked hard at their own language, at Latin, mathematics and even French. And the instructors did so well with their pupils that, in the spring of 1847, a Commission of Education, hearing of the wonderful work done at these night classes, so magnificently attended, came to examine the boys in their poor quarters and were loud in praise and admiration of what had been achieved. And, happily for Don Bosco, their admiration translated itself into action. They asked and obtained for him an annual subsidy of 300 dollars.

Chapter 4

THE DREAM FULFILLED

AS the Oratory grew, so did Don Bosco's ambitions. So many of the poor boys he met, ready as they were to work and lead good lives, had no homes and no relations. They were obliged to lodge in such dangerous surroundings and amid so much evil that the good done at the Oratory was quickly neutralized. If he had only some place where he could shelter them! He succeeded at last in renting a hayloft near the Oratory and furnished it with clean straw and a few sheets and blankets. Some nights later, when he was coming home from a visit to a sick man through the disreputable suburb that led to Valdocco, he was aware of some young roughs who seemed to be watching him. As he neared them they began to make insulting remarks about priests—"a proud and close-fisted lot." Don Bosco greeted them with a cheery good evening. "We are thirsty and we have no money," they said rudely. "Will you stand us to a drink?"

"Gladly," he said. "Come along and we will have it together."

"A good sort," they whispered.

They proceeded to the nearest tavern and sat down at a table. "What has he in mind now?" thought the tavern-keeper, who knew Don Bosco. Over their wine the youths became quite friendly.

"I wish you would do something for me," said Don Bosco.

"Certainly," they said, "what is it?"

"You have used some very bad language since I have been with you," he replied; "will you promise to stop it?"

"Sorry," they said, "it drops out sometimes from habit before we notice. We'll really try to stop."

"Come and see me on Sunday at the Oratory," he said. "It's late now, and you ought to be going home to bed."

"Home to bed!" cried some of them, "we have no home to go to." Don Bosco's heart ached.

"Let those who have a home go to it," he said, "and those who have none come with me."

The party accordingly divided, about ten of them going with Don Bosco. He took them triumphantly to his hayloft, induced them to say an Our Father and a Hail Mary, gave them sacks of straw and all the bed clothes he could spare, bade them good night and left them to sleep.

In the morning, both boys and bed clothes had vanished. This was not encouraging, but it only served to strengthen John in his resolve. Late one night, when he and his mother were at supper, they heard a knock at the door. They opened it to find a poor boy half naked and drenched from rain. They took him in, dried him and gave him food. He was a country lad, a bricklayer, who had come to Turin to get work. None could be found, and the little money he had had in his pocket was spent. He was an orphan, homeless and starving.

"Have you made your First Communion?"

"No."

"Been confirmed?"

"No."

"To Confession?"

"Yes, when mother was alive."

"What are you going to do now?"

"I don't know," he said. He began to cry, and Margaret, full of pity, cried too.

"If I were sure you were honest," said Don Bosco, "I would keep you, but others have deceived me and stolen my sheets and blankets."

"Oh, Father, I am poor, but not a thief."

"Let us keep him tonight," begged Margaret.

"Where shall we put him?"

"In the kitchen."

"Supposing he makes off with your soup-pot?"

"He won't do that."

She spoke kindly to the boy, made up a bed, and ended by bidding him say his prayers.

"I have forgotten them."

"Say them with me," she said, and they knelt together, while he repeated them after her.

The next day, Don Bosco succeeded in getting work for him. He slept and came to his meals at the Oratory. Soon others came—another little orphan whom Don Bosco found friendless and weeping in the street and took with him. "Here is another son, Mother," he said. Work was found for him too and for others. More accommodation was urgently needed. The only thing left to do was to buy Pinardi's house outright. The good man had been approached before, but hoping for a fine bargain, the man had declared he would not sell for less than 80,000 dollars. The sum was quite exorbitant; Don Bosco dropped the matter. One day Pinardi met him.

"Well, are you going to buy my house?"

"When you are ready to sell it at a reasonable price."

"Eighty thousand dollars, as I said before."

"Then we need not discuss it."

"What are you ready to offer?"

"I am told the building is worth 25 to 28,000. I will give you 30,000."

"Done," said Pinardi, and the bargain was

concluded. Don Bosco had not a cent.

His mother was anxious. "Where on earth will you get all that money?" she asked.

"Mother, dear," he said, "if you had it would you give it to me?"

"Of course I would."

"Then why suppose that God is less generous than you are?" he answered.

As a matter of fact the house was bought and paid for within a week. Don Cafasso brought him 10,000 dollars, the gift of a rich Countess, and the day after, a priest came to ask his advice as to the disposal of 20,000 given to him to spend on charity. In February, 1851, Pinardi's house was in the hands of Don Bosco, who was able to house 30 boys. He had found work for all of them, and they set off in the morning after Mass with their breakfast in their pockets. At midday they were back again, hungry as young wolves. Soup so thick that the spoon stood up in it and hunks of solid "polenta" did something to stay their appetite. The neighboring fountain provided a wholesome drink, and each boy was given five cents for dessert. The refectory was primitive; they sat on the stairs, on the ground, or on the kitchen doorstep. They washed up at the sink, and forks and spoons went into their pockets, ready for the next meal. Don Bosco, in an old apron, circulated among them, happy and smiling, seeing that all had enough—the father of the family. When they went back to their work, Margaret cleared up and then sat by the window mending, patching and darning, unless she was busy with the heavy weekly wash. Her son helped her; how useful his tailoring was coming in now! The numbers went on increasing, and so did the work. Boys will be boys, and these boys still had much to learn. The day came when even Margaret lost courage.

"John," she said, "I am at my wits' end. They hide my saucepans, they pull my washing off the lines, they trample down the poor little bits of vegetables I am trying to grow, they tear their clothes into rags and they lose the things we have got for them with so much difficulty. Let me go back to Becchi and live in peace."

For his only answer, Don Bosco pointed to the Crucifix on the wall, and there was a moment's silence. Margaret's eyes filled with tears. "You are right, John, you are right," she said, and she put on her apron.

And now her son had conceived the idea of building a church. In a dream he had had in one of his most hopeless moments, the Lady whom he had seen before had shown him this very spot at Valdocco. A church stood there, and workrooms of every kind around a large court-yard. She had led him to the church, and over the door he had read the words, "This is my house, and the place of my glory." "You will understand," she said, "when you see the reality of what you now see only in a dream."

The shed that had been used as a chapel, though it had been twice enlarged, was now far too small to hold the numbers and so low that when the Archbishop came to confirm some of the boys, it was hardly safe for him to stand up in his mitre. Moreover, as the floor had been sunk, it was very damp in wet weather. A new church was accordingly planned, to be dedicated to St. Francis de Sales, whom John had chosen as patron of the Oratory, and in the summer of 1851 the first stone was laid. By the end of the year, thanks to the contributions that came pouring in from friends and patrons, it was ready to be opened.

The government at that time was radical and intensely anticlerical. The Archbishop of Turin who had befriended Don Bosco so loyally was in exile for his fearless championship of the rights of the Church. In spite of the fact that educational orders, first and foremost the Jesuits and the Nuns of the Sacred Heart, had been driven out of Italy and their convent suppressed, Don Bosco was already planning a new building to replace the wretched old Pinardi house, and in 1852 the work was begun. Happily for him,

Rattazzi, the Minister for Home Affairs, was his friend. Tremendously impressed with the results of the Oratory training of the boys, he asked Don Bosco one day if he thought he could do anything in the prisons. It was accordingly arranged that he should give a course of lectures to 300 young convicts in the reformatory of the town, and the results were wonderful, all but one making their Easter Communion.

Filled with compassion for them, Don Bosco one day asked the warden if he might take them all into the country for a holiday. A prompt refusal resulted in an appeal to a higher official, and when he also proved obdurate, to Rattazzi himself.

"On one condition," said the Minister, "the excursion must be attended by policemen in plain clothes."

"Please not," said Don Bosco, "I must be alone and free with my boys; I will undertake the whole responsibility."

Rattazzi, anxious perhaps to see the result of such an experiment, at last gave in. On the appointed day, the city was surprised to see the prison gates open and the inhabitants pouring out in marching order. "You won't bring them back with you," said the unhopeful warden. But they had all promised Don Bosco that they would not betray his trust in them. Six young giants of exceedingly bad reputation, who had averred that they would break the head of anyone who vexed the Father, took upon themselves the duties of prefects; and the procession, headed by a donkey carrying the provisions, went off into the country.

They lunched sitting on the grass. Then after a short talk and a few prayers, Don Bosco organized games and sports in which he joined with such infectious zest that by the evening he was quite worn out. Seeing this, they insisted that he should mount the donkey, now relieved of its burden, and escorted him back in triumph, singing as they went. The warden of the prison was an astonished man when the cheery procession turned in at the gates with not one missing.

In the winter of 1857, the new building was ready and 150 boys were in residence. They were in two groups: first, those who were employed in factories or shops and who went off to work every morning and were frequently visited at their work by Don Bosco; secondly, the Latin students.

There were some among these poor little youngsters, picked up in many ways, who were more gifted than the rest—children of respectable families ruined by the war, possible vocations with no chance of realization; boys of a more delicate type, unfitted for rough work. For these, who would make good clerks if nothing else, Don Bosco planned a course of secondary education. At present, however, he had no teachers—though the day was to come when he would have them in plenty—and was obliged to send the boys into the town for the rudiments of Latin and the rest. He had many friends among the schoolmasters of Turin who were ready to take them into their classes. And so the work went on until the day when, six years later, the desire of his heart was accomplished, and he was able to teach all his boys at home.

The very necessity for making both ends meet had induced the indefatigable Don Bosco to start shoemaking and tailoring workshops in the old Pinardi house. With the new building came the possibility for a carpenter's shop and a bookbinding class; while a few years later, realizing what might be accomplished by its means, Don Bosco started a small printing press. A blacksmith's shop and other industries followed. By this time the older students had become masters and Latin classes were in full swing. The boys could be completely trained at the Oratory.

And now came a crushing blow. It looked as if his mother had been left to him just so long as her help was absolutely necessary to his undertaking. They had struggled together through dark days of abject poverty. Now the work of the

Oratory was becoming known and was winning general sympathy. Some good women of the town had even undertaken all the washing and mending of the establishment. Margaret might rest. In November of 1856, she fell ill; she would die within the week.

"Seek nothing but the glory of God," she said to her son, "and always build on the foundation of poverty." Her last words were characteristic. "John, my darling," she said, "it hurts me to see you suffer. Go to your own room and pray for me there." She looked at him, and then upwards. He understood. It was not a real goodbye since they would meet again in Heaven. A few hours later, Don Bosco was at La Consolata, his mother's favorite church, saying Mass for the repose of the soul of that valiant woman who had been his good angel all his life. "And now," he prayed to Our Lady of Consolation, "you must take her place. My great family is motherless. I give them all to you; watch over them, soul and body." His prayer was faithfully answered. Was not Our Lady the shepherdess of his dream?

It happened one day not long afterwards that Don Pacchiotti, one of the very priests who ten years before had been so anxious about Don Bosco's sanity, was invited to preach to the children in St. Francis de Sales, the church of the

Oratory. Afterwards, with some of Don Bosco's young clerics to whom he had recently given Minor Orders, Don Pacchiotti went to the refectory for a glass of wine. "Do you remember your dreams?" he asked: "a church, classes, workshops, young priests, more and more boys? We laughed; we thought you were mad—and now!"

Those ten years had been a time of great anxiety, of incessant labor and patient courage. Besides 150 boys living at Valdocco, he had 500 who came on Sundays and feast days to spend the day in the old way. He had started two more Oratories dedicated to St. Aloysius and the Guardian Angels in other parts of the town, for Valdocco was too far for some of them to come. In the winter of 1849, he conceived the idea of gathering together not only the boys of his own three houses, but any others who could be induced to come for a week's retreat, to be ended by a general Confession and Communion. They met at half-past five in the morning in a large church in a central part of the town for Mass and an instruction. During the free hour at midday they were there again for the Rosary and the kind of story-sermon broken by dialogues at which Don Bosco was such an adept and which was immensely popular. At seven, when work was over, there was another instruction and Benediction.

Before the retreat began, Don Bosco had sent

printed notices to employers begging them to
leave their young workers free at the stated times,
and where he suspected there might be opposition, he went himself to plead his cause. In spite
of the early hour and the cold, the retreat was
attended by hundreds. At the midday hour, the
crush was so great that there was hardly standing room. Throughout the week the confessionals
were crowded, and on the last evening Confessions went on well into the night. The faithful
Don Borel, with two other old friends, was helping in the enterprise, and on New Year's Eve,
when the retreat closed, the Communions seemed
never ending. One of the younger boys, a con-
scientious youth who was determined to make
a good Confession, wrote out his sins on a sheet
of paper—and lost it! He was discovered in tears
by Don Bosco.

"What is the matter, sonny?" he asked.

"I have lost my sins."

"Good business," said Don Bosco, "you will
go straight to Heaven if you have no sins."

"It's the paper where I'd written them, Father—
I can't find it."

"It is in safe hands," said Don Bosco, pulling
it out of his pocket.

The urchin was delighted. "If I'd known it
was you who had them, Father, I should just
have said, 'Father, I accuse myself of all the sins

you have in your pocket.'"

In the summer of 1854, there was a terrible outbreak of cholera in Turin, and Valdocco was one of the worst points in the city. The Town Council had opened two hospitals in the most infected quarters, but the question remained: who was to seek out and bring in isolated cases, for too often, at the first sign of the disease, the victims were abandoned by their terrified relations. Don Bosco, who was everywhere at once, caring for both the bodies and souls of the dying, realized immediately the necessity of a band of devoted workers. He appealed to his elder boys, 40 of whom signed up, and organized a plan of action. Some worked in the hospitals, others in private houses, some explored the workmen's premises to seek out cases abandoned by the rest. A small group held themselves in readiness at the Oratory for any need that might arise by day or by night.

For three months, while the scourge lasted, they worked incessantly, and not one succumbed to the dreaded disease. In the early days, they had orders to use all necessary precautions, to wash and change whenever they came in, but at the height of the epidemic this became impossible. Their trust in the protection of Our Lady was their only defense. Many of the poor creatures whom they found in attics and cellars were in a state of utter destitution. All the reserves of house linen at the Oratory had to be commandeered—the boys were ready to give up everything but what they had on their backs. The work required courage. There were horrible sights to be faced. One lad fainted at his first experience of nursing. But Don Bosco was there to revive and encourage, and they held on. Good people in the town, and some who could not be included in that category, were united in praise of the devoted work that had been done.

Not Turin alone, but the whole of Piedmont was ringing with Don Bosco's praises. He was in demand for missions, retreats and sermons everywhere. His had no great eloquence or oratorical splendor. He spoke quietly and simply, with intense conviction, of the great truths of the Faith. He never mentioned topical subjects and never touched on politics or on the questions of the day. He preached the Gospel, and he himself was the most powerful sermon of all.

It is still remembered how, when he came to preach the triduum preparatory to the feast of the Assumption in Montemagno, in the midst of a terrible drought which threatened the ruin of vines, grain and vegetables, he promised rain if all the people would put their trust in Our Lady and make their peace with God. "You're a bold man," said the parish priest afterwards, "very bold. To promise rain for the Feast of the Assumption."

"What! I didn't say that, did I?"

"Indeed you did. Ask the sacristan; they all believe you, too."

The church at Montemagno had never held such crowds; the people were packed like sardines at every instruction, and Confessions never stopped. "You're sure it will rain?" they asked whenever they met the preacher. "Go on praying," was the invariable answer.

The sun rose on the Feast of the Assumption more brilliant than ever. Don Bosco began to wonder if he had not been tempting Providence. The bell rang for the afternoon instruction; it was sunnier than ever. "What shall I say to them," he thought, "if Our Lady does not come to my help?"

"A complete fiasco, my poor Don Bosco," said the priest, meeting him on the way. "How you are going to get out of it, I don't know."

"John," said Don Bosco to the sacristan, like Elias of old, "go out and see if there is not a cloud somewhere."

"Nothing but a tiny one on the horizon," said he a minute later, "but it won't come to anything."

"Give me the stole," said Don Bosco, and went into the church.

"Blessed Mother Mary," he prayed, "it is not my honor that is at stake, but yours. What will these people think, who have been praying so hard to induce you to send them rain?"

The *Magnificat* had been sung, and he went toward the pulpit. The church was so jammed that he could hardly reach it. He began his sermon; the sky grew dark. He went on, and it grew darker still. Before he was well into it, a clap of thunder shook the building; another and another followed. The rain fell, steadily and softly, while the preacher, with his heart full of gratitude, spoke of the confidence which every Christian ought to have in the intercession of God's most Blessed Mother. When Benediction was over, the congregation had a long time to wait before there was enough lull in the downpour to make possible a dash for home.

But it was among his boys that Don Bosco was in his real element. He never forgot the words of his mother: "God sees you, He knows even your most secret thoughts"—and the effect this teaching had had on his own impetuous youth. He was convinced that the virtues of the Christian life must come from within, not from without. Hence, love and confidence in God and frequent recourse to the Sacraments of the Church must be at the base of all good efforts. He remembered, too, how the reserved manner of

some of the priests he had known had chilled
his own young heart and how he had longed to
find among them a friend to whom he could
pour out his aspirations, his difficulties and his
trials. He was that friend to his boys, and he
made his own young priests follow in his foot-
steps. Punishment and coercion were abhorrent
to him. He believed with St. Francis de Sales,
his patron, that one can do more with a spoon-
ful of honey than with a barrel of vinegar.

A happy freedom reigned in his Oratories,
where priests and masters, always in the midst
of the boys, ready with a word of help, encouragement or warning, were loved and trusted by
all. Don Bosco had so long been accustomed to
hearing the Confessions of his children in the
open air at the side of a ditch or on a grassy
bank that he had no devotion to the enclosed
confessional, sometimes alarming to the very
young. The boys knelt beside him, his fatherly
arm around their shoulders, and told him all
they had to tell. Then followed a little talk, heart
to heart, and with the grace of the Sacrament
on their souls, they would run off lighthearted
and happy. He had the gift of reading hearts
and would sometimes gently mention something
that the young penitent had omitted. The boys
believed that if they had done wrong he could
read it on their faces. Perhaps he could. One

night in the dormitory a boy was weeping.

"What on earth is the matter?" asked his friend. "Don Bosco looked at me today."

"Well! He looked at me, too."

"Yes, but if you had seen his eyes when he looked at me!"

The next day the boy's friend met Don Bosco.

"What was the matter with so-and-so yesterday?" he asked.

"Oh, he knows very well," was the answer.

The discipline at the Oratory was not for show, it was individual—for the will. Don Bosco believed that boys should be allowed to make noise—as much as they liked—at recreation. He believed in life and joy and movement. Sometimes he would line up his six or 700 boys and march them off at a lively gait, singing a folk song of old Piedmont in which they eagerly joined, keeping in step and marking the time by a vigorous clapping of hands. In and out they went, up a staircase, down a long corridor, around and around in serpentine twistings, delirious with excitement. The din was absolutely deafening; so was the tramping of hundreds of strong young feet, but when legs and voices were weary and they stopped for lack of breath, they had thoroughly enjoyed life. Even classes were enjoyable. The boys were expected to work seriously, but there were compensations. A theater was one of

Don Bosco's earliest enterprises. Plays were acted, historical episodes presented, and music was always to the fore. The choir of the Oratory was in demand for festive occasions all over the city. A choir of boys' voices was a novelty in Italy at that time and provoked much admiration.

"Without confidence and love," Don Bosco would say, "there can be no true education." He himself was a living example. "If you want to be loved," he told his disciples, "you yourselves must love, and make your children feel that you love them." Unwearying patience with the least responsive, a loving vigilance to defend them from themselves, a tenderness that persists in spite of all rebuffs, a trust that cannot but call out response—these were the principles on which he worked and taught others to work with him.

For the boys, the Holy Eucharist and devotion to God's holy Mother were to be their strength and support in all temptations. For the teaching and training of boys and young people, Don Bosco certainly had most wonderful gifts; first of all, perhaps, his most charming and attractive personality. He was discussing one day the subject of education with Cardinal Tosti on the occasion of his first visit to Rome. "You can do nothing," he said, "with young people unless you have their confidence and love."

"How do you get it?"

"By doing one's utmost to win their friendship."

"By what means?"

"By putting oneself in contact with them, by being like one of themselves. I will show you, if you will take me to a place where we can find some children."

The Cardinal ordered his carriage and they drove to the Piazza del Popolo where a quantity of street urchins were playing together. Don Bosco got out and the Cardinal watched. At the approach of the priest the children fled, but in no way discouraged, he called them gently back, and a few, rather cautiously at first, obeyed the call. He felt in his pockets, produced some sweets and began to chat with them. At the sight of his kindly smile and disarming friendliness, the rest came back, till presently they were all there.

"Suppose you begin your game again," he said after a while, "and I will play with you."

He tucked up his cassock and the game began, noisily and with great zest. At the sight of this wonderful priest who played games with children, others who came to look joined in, and all were welcomed with a kind word.

I must go now," he said, giving them each a medal. "Say your prayers and go to Confession like good children."

"Oh, don't go," they begged, clinging onto him; "don't go, stay with us!"

The Cardinal was convinced.

Chapter 5

A MIGHTY ENTERPRISE

"A CHURCH, workshops, more and more boys, plenty of priests," Don Bosco had said, and the verdict of his friends had been that he was mad. The church and the workshops and the boys were there, and he had not lost sight of the rest. It was absolutely necessary that he should have priests to help him in the work, and preferably priests of his own training. The little group of his older boys whom he had taught and trained with a view to possible vocations disappointed his expectations. A second group did the same. He then turned to the young priests of Turin who were always ready to help him, in the hope of forming the nucleus of a little community. But a short experience of the stark renunciation required by the work proved too much for their courage. Again he reverted to his first idea. Among his older boys he picked out four.

"Would you like to be my helpers at the Oratory?" he asked them.

"How could we be your helpers?"

"In many ways. I would complete your education, and perhaps one day you might become priests. Who knows? Do you like the idea?"

They did like it, and set to work with all their might, with such success that in the spring of 1851, with the approbation of Archbishop Franzoni, then in exile, he sent one of the clerical students to the university. Two failed to persevere, and the other two entered the diocesan seminary. He had failed again. But Don Bosco was not an easy man to discourage. Passing through the great marketplace of Turin, he met one day a boy of ten, Michael Rua, on his way to school. The boy, who knew Don Bosco, asked him for a medal. In answer, Don Bosco, holding out his open right hand, pretended to cut it in two with his left. "There you are, Michael," he said. "What does he mean?" the child asked himself. Years later, when he the young man was ordained a deacon, Don Bosco explained. "Michael," he said, "you will be my other half."

Rua was soon joined by others: Cagliero, who was later to be bishop and Cardinal; Francesia, Turchi, Bonetti, all boys of the Oratory or young peasants from the country. On June 5, 1852, after night prayers, Don Bosco called these young disciples to his room and proposed his plan. They were to be his staff, his *aides-de-camp*, always to second him in the work. Two years later, in January, 1854, during the novena to St. Francis de Sales, the little troop was given a name. They were to be Salesians, bound by a promise that later might resolve itself into a vow. St. Francis, incessant worker for souls, apostle of joy, model of courtesy and patient charity, intrepid defender of the Faith, had always been John Bosco's hero. To him the new religious family was to be dedicated. The novitiate now began, private but strenuous, and a year later, before a crucifix in Don Bosco's room, Don Rua, the first of a great line, took the vows of religion. The Salesian Order was born.

It was a moment for caution. A government intensely hostile to the Church was doing everything in its power to throw discredit on priests, religious orders and everything connected with Catholic worship, and it was not till 1857 that the constitutions and rules of the new Society were submitted for approval to the Holy See.

It was about this time that the government minister Rattazzi, still friendly to Don Bosco, told him that he hoped he would live to be a very old man. "Still," he said, "we are not immortal. What will happen to your work when you are no longer here? Have you thought of that?"

Don Bosco was silent.

"You ought to associate more closely with

yourself some of those young men and young priests who are helping you so ably at Valdocco and form a society to carry on the work."

Don Bosco smiled. "Your Excellency," he said. "You! Talking about a Congregation! When the laws—"

"Oh, laws," said the minister, "I know all about that; they are directed at the old orders. Make a society that is nothing more than an association of free citizens and you'll be all right. After all, it's a work of benevolence and general utility."

"I will think about it," said Don Bosco.

In February, 1858, he was in Rome with Don Rua. Pope Pius IX was full of interest in his work.

"But if you were to die, what would happen?" he asked, repeating Rattazzi's question.

"It is to speak to you about that that I have come to Rome, Your Holiness."

Twelve days later Don Bosco, at a second audience, placed in the hands of the Pope the manuscript of rules and constitutions that he had drawn up. The first step was taken, and on his return to Turin, the first council of the Salesian Congregation was held. In 1862, the 24 first disciples of Don Bosco vowed themselves to the service of the Society: Don Michael Rua, who was to succeed him as head of the Order, Don

Cagliero, who was to become Cardinal, Don Albera, who was to be the third Superior General, and others who were to hold important charges.

"My sons," said Don Bosco, "we are living in troublous times, when it looks like folly to found a new religious order. But God has blessed our work and will go on blessing it. The very fact that it has had to surmount so many difficulties is a reason for confidence. We seek God's glory and the good of souls alone. Who knows that He may not use this humble congregation to do great things in His world?"

His words, as often before, were prophetic.

The son on whom Don Bosco had based his highest hopes was helping from Heaven. Young Dominic Savio was the rather rare type of boy who seemed to have a natural attraction for everything that is good and beautiful. Don Bosco met him in the year of the cholera epidemic at Castelnuovo; Dominic came to the Oratory, where he remained till his death three years later. Dominic offered himself at once as instructor of the younger boys in catechism and religious doctrine. Unselfishness and devotedness were characteristic of him. Some of the older boys had banded themselves together to help and influence the more unruly of their companions. Of this league, Dominic was the leader and the soul.

He passed among the boys like a clean wind: dark faces cleared and smiles broke out. He was the hero of all the rascals in the school, who were always at his heels; he had something of Don Bosco's own irresistible joyousness. There were others, too, whom he persistently sought out and befriended; they were the most uncouth and ignorant of the boys, those who were the least attractive and the least popular—and most of all, those who were the most careless about their religious duties. After a walk or a game with one of these he would say, "I am going to Confession tomorrow, will you come?" And he would bring with him five or six companions. "Dominic catches more fish with his little games," Don Bosco would say, "than many preachers with their sermons." The boy had a great gift of prayer and a strange supernatural knowledge of passing events.

"Please come with me," he said one day to Don Bosco; "you are needed badly and very quickly." Don Bosco, who had had experience of the boy's strange intuitions, followed him to a tenement house.

"They want you up there," said Dominic, pointing to a window on the third floor. Don Bosco went up—to be met by a woman.

"Quick," she said, "or you will be too late. My husband is dying; he is a Protestant and he wants to be reconciled to the Church." Don Bosco had just time to hear the man's Confession and prepare him for death.

"I wish I could see the Holy Father," said Dominic one day to Don Bosco.

"What would you say to him?"

"Oh, I know that he is praying for England and I could tell him something that would give him joy. The other day when I was making my thanksgiving after Communion, it seemed to me that I saw in a strange country a great light shining on a crowd of people who seemed to have lost their way in the darkness. The light came from the hand of the Holy Father, and when it shone on them, the darkness drifted and it was daylight. Then someone beside me said: 'The light is the Catholic Faith, which is to enlighten England.'"

It was noticed one day that Dominic looked ill, and the doctor advised rest in his own home town. His father came to fetch him home, but Dominic did not want to go.

"I want to end my days at the Oratory," he said.

"There is no question of ending your days," they said. "You will go home and come back well and strong."

"No," said Dominic, "I shall not come back."

After a week or two, the doctor congratulated

him on his improvement, but the boy asked for the last Sacraments; and to please him, his request was granted. He was radiant.

"Take my prayer book, Father," he said, "and read the prayers for the dying." When his father came to the words, "Receive me into Thy bosom, that I may sing Thy praises forever," Dominic said, "yes, that is what I long for, to sing His praises forever," and crossing his hands on his breast, with a loving smile at his father, he gave up his soul to God. The perfume of his young life remained an inspiration in the Salesian family. Dominic Savio was proclaimed a Saint of the Church by Pope Pius XII on June 12, 1954.

The Waldensians, who had established themselves fairly strongly in Turin, started a campaign of propaganda, and Don Bosco, with the aid of his printing press, took up the cudgels for the Church. The logic and vigor of his papers and pamphlets did such good work in refuting the errors of his adversaries that they vowed vengeance against him. One night, as he was giving the usual catechism lesson to his boys, he was shot at through the window, the bullet passing between his body and his arm. The boys were terrified.

"Come," said he, "go on with your lesson. That was a bad shot; the worst of it is that my best soutane has been torn."

Another evening, he was sent for to visit a dying man. He called two of his biggest boys to go with him. "There is no need of them," said the messenger. "We will take you."

"I want to give these boys a breath of fresh air," said Don Bosco, and off they went.

In the basement of the house some forbidding-looking men were drinking.

"Wait here a moment," said one of the two who had fetched him, "while I go to prepare the invalid."

"Will you have some chestnuts, Father?" asked one of the drinkers.

"No, thank you," said Don Bosco.

"Then a little wine?"

"No, thank you."

"Come, just to please us," said the man, and he filled a glass out of a bottle standing by itself on a shelf.

"No, thank you."

"What! You insult us!" said another threateningly. "If you don't drink it willingly, you shall be made to drink it."

"Perhaps one of my young men will take it," said Don Bosco, who had opened the door and beckoned to his escort.

"No, no," said the man, hastily snatching the glass, "it is you to whom it was offered and not to these boys."

This looked suspicious. Don Bosco rose and demanded to see the sick man. He was taken up to a room where under a heap of bedclothes lay one of the two rascals who had come to fetch him. At sight of the priest he burst into a roar of insulting laughter.

"I'll go to Confession another time!" he shouted.

Once more, in the summer of 1855, the incident repeated itself. He was asked to give the last Sacraments to a woman. It was a dark night, and remembering his recent adventure, he took four boys with him, two of whom were big and strong. The house was in a lonely part of the town. Two of them waited downstairs while the other two went up to the door of the room where the sick woman was supposed to be. Don Bosco went in, to be greeted with feigned cordiality by four unpleasant-looking men armed with stout sticks. He approached the bed, where the invalid was breathing heavily; for a dying woman she had wonderful color. With a request to the men to move away, Don Bosco asked the woman if she were ready for Confession.

"I will do nothing," she shouted, "till that great brute over there, my brother-in-law, begs my pardon." And she burst into a torrent of abuse.

"Will you hold your tongue, you wretch!"

cried one of the men and promptly put out the only candle. At the same moment a blow was aimed at Don Bosco that would have brained him had he not stepped aside. He seized a chair and, holding it over his head to ward off the blows that were raining upon him, made for the door, flung the chair back at his assailants, rejoined his boys and soon was safely in the street.

Attempts on himself he could forgive, but it was different when it was a matter of seducing his little protégés, some of whom were too weak to resist a propaganda backed by bribes. Word came to him one day that one of his old boys who had joined the Waldensians was dying and longing to be reconciled to the Church. He had implored his mother to bring him a priest, but the priest had been refused admittance by the Waldensians, on guard day and night. Don Bosco set off at once with two of his most sturdy boys. He was stopped at the door by a man.

"What do you want?"

"I want to see the patient."

"Quite impossible; the doctor's orders are definite. The slightest excitement might be fatal."

"Come, let me pass, I have no time to waste; I will say a word to the mother, and then I will go. Why, there she is! Good morning, my good woman, how is your son?" And Don Bosco advanced steadily toward the door of the sick-room.

"Did you not hear me?" asked the man. "Go away! There is no admittance."

As his only answer, Don Bosco pushed him aside and opened the door.

"Oh, Don Bosco, Don Bosco!" cried the sick boy eagerly, "do come in!"

"For the last time, will you go!" protested the man. "That boy is inscribed on our books."

"For more than ten years he has been inscribed on mine," was the answer, "but let him decide the question. Peter," he said, turning to the boy, "what do you want?"

"I was born a Catholic," said the boy, "and I repent with all my heart of what I have done."

There was no more to be said. Don Bosco sat down to comfort the lad and to give him back his peace of soul. In 24 hours he was dead.

Don Bosco was a firm believer in the power of the press and did not content himself with papers and leaflets. He wrote a history of Italy for the use of schools and a manual of mathematics. A prayerbook and another manual of Christian doctrine followed—which could hardly be printed fast enough, so greatly was it in demand. *Catholic Readings*, a monthly publication, provided a timely antidote to the writings circulated against the Church and was immensely popular. In spite of his absorbing work at the Oratory, Don Bosco, by making use of the hours of the night, contrived to do a great deal of writing.

The Congregation was growing steadily, and Don Bosco undertook a second journey to Rome to plead his cause and to ask for a final approbation from the Holy See. The new Archbishop of Turin, however, hoping to find in Don Bosco's enterprise a nursery of parish priests for the diocese, was by no means pleased to find it the nucleus of a religious Congregation. Orders were issued that Don Bosco was not to use for the work of the Oratory any priests who were natives of the archdiocese and was to present for Orders only young men who had been trained in the diocesan seminary.

"My Lord Archbishop," he protested, "it will be the ruin of my work. I shall be left to cope with it unaided."

"I cannot help it, my dear Don Bosco. It is in the interests of my young priests that I insist."

"Let us refer it to Rome," pleaded Don Bosco.

"No need," was the reply; "it is a little difference that we can easily settle between us."

A little difference! It went on for years and it threatened the very existence of his life's work. At Rome, too, there had been reports which created uneasiness. The religious were too few, the rules were too simple and the poverty of the enterprise was not very reassuring. Don Bosco received a letter from Archbishop Svegliati, Secretary of the Congregation of Regulars, which made him decide to set off for Rome at once. His friends were against it. "It is not a good moment," they said. "There have been unfavorable and unjust reports, and they have not been without effect. Wait till the Vatican Council is over."

In Rome, Don Bosco soon realized that there was much against him and that very few of the most influential churchmen were in his favor. There remained to him the weapon of prayer.

Cardinal Berardi, one of his strongest adversaries, had a little nephew who was dying of typhoid, an only son and heir to a great fortune. Don Bosco was begged to visit him, and he went.

"Obtain his cure for us," begged the parents.

"Have confidence in Our Lady, Help of Christians," he replied, "and let us begin a novena in her honor."

He began it on the spot, blessed the sick child and left the house. To the astonishment of all, the fever vanished, and three days later when Don Bosco went back to see him, the boy was sitting up in bed, laughing and talking, well on the way to recovery. Father, mother and uncle were overjoyed.

"What can I do for you, my dear Don Bosco?" asked the Cardinal.

"Just one thing," was the answer. "Use your influence with the Holy Father for the approval of my little Congregation."

"I will," said the Cardinal, and he kept his word.

That was at least one victory, but it was not enough. "If only I could get hold of the Cardinal Secretary of State," thought Don Bosco, and he set off to his house. Cardinal Antonelli, prostrate with a bad attack of gout, received him kindly.

"I would gladly do what I could for you," he said, "but you see my condition."

"Do it all the same," said Don Bosco, "and I know you will get better."

"What is it you want?"

"Speak in our favor to the Holy Father."

"I'd do it gladly, Don Bosco, but I can't stir a step."

"Trust in Our Lady, Help of Christians, and you will soon be all right; but don't forget the poor Salesian Congregation."

"I promise I won't. As soon as I can crawl, I'll go to the Holy Father."

"Tomorrow, then?"

"Tomorrow! You don't know what you are talking about!"

"Yes I do; trust in Our Lady, and you will be all right."

The next morning, Cardinal Antonelli was so much better that he could walk. In the afternoon the pain had gone, and he hurried off to the Pope to tell him what had happened and to keep his promise. A few days later, Pius IX sent for Don Bosco, and they had a long talk together.

"I think it will be all right," said the Pope, "if you can win over Archbishop Svegliati. He is your most formidable enemy. If you gain him, the opposition will be broken."

A few hours later, Don Bosco was in the antechamber of the Secretary of the Congregation of Bishops and Regulars, to find him in bed with a sharp attack of influenza.

"How unfortunate, Your Excellency," he said. "I came to ask your help in a pressing emergency. I want you to smooth out the difficulties in the way of the approbation of my Society."

"Not so easy, Don Bosco," was the reply. "You see the condition I am in."

"All the same, Your Excellency, I am in dire need of you. I want you to see the Holy Father, who seems favorably disposed toward us."

"But how can I?"

"How? I will tell you. Recommend yourself to Our Lady, Help of Christians, and promise her to do your best for the poor little Salesian

Congregation. You will soon be well."

"You speak with great confidence!"

"Try it, Your Excellency, and you will see. Trust in Our Lady."

"Well, Don Bosco, look here. If I am able to go to the Holy Father tomorrow, I promise to speak in your favor."

The next morning Archbishop Svegliati had stopped coughing. His temperature was normal, and he was as well as usual. After his audience with the Holy Father, he came to tell Don Bosco that when the question of the Congregation came up for discussion, he could count on his support.

On the day appointed for the conference, the boys at Turin were succeeding each other before the altar in one long chain of prayer, and their prayers were answered. A decree was passed approving the Congregation and giving Don Bosco, for a period of ten years, the right of presenting for Orders, solely for service in the Society, any candidates who had been received into the Oratory before their 14th year. The definitive approbation of the Rule was postponed till later. With the brief in his pocket, Don Bosco set out for home. It was not yet complete victory, but it was enough to go on for now. Some ten years later came the longed-for approbation of the Rule.

Don Bosco had never forgotten the church of his dream which Our Lady herself had shown to him. The Church of St. Francis de Sales, which had seemed so vast when it was built, was already much too small for the crowds who came to it. At the 9 o'clock Mass on Sunday, when everyone was in it, the walls were bursting, and in its immediate neighborhood were districts where there was no church at all. One night in the winter of 1862, when he had been hearing Confessions until late at night, he went at about 11 o'clock to supper with one of his first disciples. To the astonishment of his companion, he—usually so gay and cheery—seemed tired, preoccupied and absent.

"I have heard so many Confessions," he said at last, "that in the end I did not know what I was saying or doing, and all the time I had one thought in my mind: when shall we build a larger church—the Church of Our Lady, Help of Christians? Ours is much too small. I know it's a great enterprise and I haven't a penny. Still, if the Lord wants it, He will have it."

"It has been a beautiful day," he said a few days later to Don Cagliero on the Feast of the Immaculate Conception. "It is on this day that most of our works have been inaugurated. But Our Lady wishes us now to honor her especially under the title of Help of Christians. In these evil days we need her help. It is to her, under this title, that I intend to build a church—and for another reason too. Can you guess it?"

"To be the mother-church of the Congregation," was the prompt reply.

"Yes. Our Lady, Help of Christians will be the Foundress and perpetual Protectress of all our works."

"Where will you build it?" asked Don Anfossi.

"Here, beside the Church of St. Francis de Sales," said Don Bosco with a wide sweep of the arm.

"As big as that?"

"Yes. People will come from far and near to honor Our Lady and invoke her powerful help."

"Where will the money come from?"

"Our Lady will see to that; it is her church."

The first obstacle came from the owners of the land where it was proposed to build. Then came the objection of the municipal council. They did not mind the erection of a church, but they objected strongly to the title. It sounded as if the Christians were appealing for help against the government. To counteract all this, Don Bosco refrained, in all his plans, from giving the church a name. The foundations were dug in the spring of 1863. The purchase of the site had swallowed up every available penny, and when the first sod was dug, the cashbox was empty.

"I do not have the money for a stamp to send off the mail," groaned the bursar.

"Go on all the same," said Don Bosco; "did you ever see me with money when I began anything? We must leave something to Providence."

Providence provided. But the next year when the walls were beginning to rise, the cashbox was empty again.

"Give me something to pay the workmen," said the builder.

"Take all I have," answered Don Bosco, emptying his money into the man's hand. Eight cents fell out; the builder was aghast.

"Don't be afraid," said Don Bosco, "Our Lady will send us all that is necessary. I am only her banker; it will be all right."

And it was, but not without frequent anxieties. During the five years that went to its building, the work had to be held up more than once. Don Bosco was a firm believer in the truth that God helps those who help themselves, and he worked unceasingly. First it was a huge lottery authorized by the government; then a circular letter addressed to all lovers of Our Lady; then an appeal to princes, subscribers for bricks, etc. Finally, at the end of all his resources, he set off on a pilgrimage through Italy to solicit funds, and it was richly rewarded. Then when human means were exhausted, there was the unfailing power of prayer. "There is hardly a stone in the building," he would say later, "that does not represent a grace from Our Lady."

One day, when it was a question of giving up the famous dome on which Don Bosco had set his heart, he went to see a wealthy old friend who was very ill.

"I am very ill, Don Bosco. I am dying."

"Not a bit of it," replied Don Bosco. "What would you do if Our Lady, Help of Christians were to give you back your health and strength?"

"I would give you 500 dollars for six consecutive months for your church."

"Courage and confidence," was the reply. "I will go home and set my boys to praying."

Three days later when Don Bosco was busy writing letters, the door opened. There stood the dying man, full of life and health. He had insisted on bringing the first installment himself.

Another time, in November 1866, a bill for 8,000 dollars was due to be paid that night, and Don Bosco had nothing to pay it with. Don Rua, bursar to the little Congregation, went out with one or two companions to see what could be done. They came back—having exhausted every possibility—with 2,000 dollars and looked at each other in despair. Don Bosco smiled.

"Come to dinner, and afterwards I will go for the rest," he said.

At 1 o'clock he set off, praying quietly for help, and walked on with no specific aim till he found himself close to the principal station of the city. There he stopped, wondering where to go next, when he was suddenly accosted by a servant in livery.

"I beg your pardon, Father, but are you not Don Bosco?"

"Yes, what can I do for you?"

"My master would like to see you at once."

"Where does he live?"

"There," pointing to a large and handsome house. "He is very rich, he might be able to do something for your church."

In a spacious and beautifully furnished apartment, an elderly gentleman was in bed.

"Reverend Father," he said, "I have great need of your prayers. I think they will cure me."

"Have you been ill long?"

"For three years. I am in great pain and unable to move—the doctors give me no hope. If you could do something for me, I would give you an offering for your church."

"This is the hand of God," said Don Bosco. "I am in urgent need of 6,000 dollars."

"Six thousand dollars! You don't know what you are talking about! If it were 1,000 dollars I might perhaps be able to do something."

"Too much?" asked Don Bosco, "then we'll

drop the subject," and sitting down beside the sick man, he began to talk of current affairs.

"But Father, that doesn't matter, it is my cure that I want to talk about."

"Your cure? I mentioned means, and you were not inclined to take them."

"Six thousand dollars!"

"I am not pressing you."

"Look here, pray that I get better, and at the end of the year I will see what I can do for you."

"The end of the year! But I must have the sum by this evening."

"This evening! Impossible! I should have to go to the bank."

"And why not?"

"I have not been out of bed for three years—it's quite impossible."

"Nothing is impossible to God and His Blessed Mother," said Don Bosco.

He had all the servants summoned, bade them join him in prayer, and then ordered them to bring their master's clothes. Their master's clothes! Where were they? It had been three years since he had worn them.

"Go and get them," said Don Bosco.

The doctor now came in and declared that they were all insane. In the meantime, clothes had been brought, and the invalid, having dressed himself, began to stride about the room.

"Let me have a bite," he ordered in great delight, "and bring the carriage around."

Shortly afterwards, he appeared before Don Bosco with the required sum.

"I am entirely cured," he said.

"You have taken your money out of the bank," said Don Bosco, "and Our Lady has taken you out of bed."

And so, by dint of faith, labor and prayer, the great church advanced to completion. When the last stone was to crown the edifice, Don Bosco determined that the hand of a child should place it. Before a huge multitude of spectators, he climbed the ladders that led to the apex of the building with a little boy, the son of one of his greatest benefactors, and to a shout of acclamation the last stone slipped into its place.

Chapter 6

THE WAYS OF A SAINT

IN SPITE of the hundreds of boys who belonged to the Sunday Oratory or who were in residence at Valdocco, there were others who had not yet been tracked down by this hunter of souls. The leader of a certain gang of young scamps who used to meet regularly was astonished one day at the absence of one of their number.

"Where can he be?" he asked.

"Oh, I know," said another, "he has gone to Don Bosco's Oratory."

"What on earth is that?"

"Oh, they say it's a place where boys meet and run about and play, and pray and sing and go to church."

"Run about and play—that would suit me. Where is it?"

"At Valdocco."

The boy set off. The door was shut, for they were all in the chapel, but he climbed onto the wall and jumped down into the yard. An Oratory boy passing on his way to the church invited the stranger in with him. Don Borel was in the middle of one of his inimitable sermons on sheep and wolves and was showing how the sheep were those who were trying to lead a good life and the wolves were bad companions who tried to lead them astray.

"Avoid bad companions," he said, "those who blaspheme and steal and do not fear God. Here in the Oratory you are in the sheepfold, where strong watchdogs are on guard to defend and take care of you. Come often to the Oratory on Sundays and feast days and you will be safe from the attacks of wolves."

The stranger had never heard a sermon that was so simple and practical; he understood it all. When it was over the boys sang the Litany of the Blessed Virgin, and as he liked singing, he joined in.

"Who is Don Bosco?" he asked his friend when they came out. "Was it the one who preached?"

"No," said the boy. "Come along and I will take you to him."

Don Bosco was in the playground, surrounded by a crowd of boys. He gave the newcomer a hearty welcome and invited him to join in the games.

"I saw you and heard you singing," he said;

"you have a good voice and I would like to teach you."

A few kindly words won the boy's heart completely. He began to come to the Oratory regularly and brought all his friends with him. His parents, however, of the anti-clerical type, protested strongly and beat the boy when he insisted that at the Oratory he was taught nothing but good. They began to treat him so cruelly that at last he ran to Don Bosco for protection. The parents followed, furious.

"I shall go to the magistrates," said the father, and they will help me to drag my boy out of the clutches of you priests."

"I will go with you," said Don Bosco promptly, "and testify to your treatment of your son."

This did not appeal to them at all. They went off, rather alarmed, and the boy became a pupil at the Oratory. Musical and very intelligent, he began to learn rapidly and ended by becoming a priest and the Oratory organist.

One day when Don Bosco had gone to a barber shop for a shave, he caught sight of a young apprentice, a little boy of 11, and began to make friends with him.

"Have you made your First Communion?" he asked.

"No."

"Do you go to catechism class?"

"Sometimes, when I can."

"That's good. Now I want you to shave me."

"No! Wait!" cried the barber in alarm; "he is only learning."

"He will never learn if he doesn't practice," said Don Bosco. "Come on, my boy!"

"If you don't mind," protested the barber, "I would prefer him not to learn on a priest."

"But I want him to shave me," said Don Bosco.

After a rather painful quarter of an hour he got up.

"You will become a famous barber," he said, and invited the little apprentice to come to the Oratory on the following Sunday. There he prepared him for Confession, and soon after, when by the death of his mother he was left an orphan, took him in and brought him up at the Oratory.

The districts which surrounded Valdocco were, as we have seen, not particularly reputable. Don Bosco found a great field for apostleship among the shady characters who were constantly to be found drinking in the public houses or fighting outside them. As the great feasts of the Church drew near, he would spend more time with them, begging them to come to Confession and make their peace with God.

"Come whenever you like, whenever you can, my dear children," he would say; "you will find me always ready, even in the middle of the night. And, when our business is done—well, we have a little wine up there, and we will drink your health together."

Many hardened sinners were won by that lovable and persistent kindness, by that understanding of human weakness and belief that in the most unpromising characters there was always, somewhere, a vein of good.

Whenever Don Bosco went on a journey, he generally contrived to get a seat beside the coachman. He would chat with him pleasantly on all sorts of subjects and gradually bring the conversation around to the state of his soul. It generally ended in a promise to go to Confession—sometimes, even, a Confession on the spot. One day on the way to Castiglione, he asked the driver if he had been to his Easter duties.

"No," said the man, "it's a long time since I was at Confession, but, my word, if I could find the last priest I went to, I'd go like a shot."

"Who was he?"

"Don Bosco, at Turin. Perhaps you've heard of him?"

Don Bosco laughed. "Here you are," he said.

The man stared at him. "Why, of course, I never recognized you. But I can't go to Confession now, like this, can I?"

"Why not? Give me the reins." And while the

horses trotted on complacently, the driver poured out his soul to his companion.

Another day, when Don Bosco was coming back in the early morning from saying Mass in a church on the opposite side of the town, he saw four rough-looking men coming toward him. As he attempted to pass, they stood in front of him in a rather threatening manner. There was not a soul in sight.

"Here," said one of them, "we're having an argument; decide who's right."

"Come, decide," said another, without a word as to the subject of the discussion. They were evidently determined to pick a quarrel, and they were four to one.

"My good friends," said Don Bosco, "this is not the place for an argument, out here in the wild. Come into town with me, and let us talk it out over a cup of hot coffee."

"Who's going to pay for it?"

"I, of course, since I gave the invitation."

The five accordingly set off together, and it was not long before they were chatting away quite amiably.

"Look," said Don Bosco, "here is a church; let us go and say a Hail Mary before we have our coffee."

"That's an excuse to get off," growled one of them.

"Not at all," said Don Bosco; "it's not much to ask of you."

"I know your tricks—you'll begin with a Hail Mary, and the whole Rosary will come tumbling after it."

"I said a Hail Mary," was the answer, "and I meant it. Come on."

He bundled the unwilling four into the church and said the Hail Mary, in which they, more or less, joined in.

"Now we will have our coffee," said the priest. Over it, they became friendly again.

"Now we have made each other's acquaintance," said Don Bosco as he paid the bill. "Come along to my place and have something to eat."

They went in, and he turned to them suddenly.

"How long is it since you were at the Sacraments?" he asked. "If you were to die tonight, how would it be?"

They looked at each other dubiously, and one burst out:

"Oh, Don Bosco, if all priests were like you, we wouldn't mind going to Confession."

"Well, here I am," was the answer.

"We're not prepared."

"Leave that to me."

He took them one by one into his room, and

all but the last made a good Confession and a hearty purpose of amendment. He refused on the ground that he did not feel inclined; but they all went off thanking Don Bosco gratefully and promising to come again.

Another time at nightfall, in a lonely place, a suspicious-looking individual intercepted him and demanded his money-purse. Don Bosco answered him kindly, asking what unhappy circumstances had led him to actions which in his conscience he knew to be wrong. Little by little, he drew out of him the whole miserable story until, passing a little wall, Don Bosco sat down on it, while the man on his knees beside him proceeded to make his Confession. It was a dark corner, but a canon of the cathedral, passing in the vicinity, was aware of the two shadowy figures. "Ah," he said to himself, "there's Don Bosco at his usual work."

There was at the Oratory a big boy of 16 named Albert. He had begun well, but had been led astray by a bad companion and was a source of great anxiety to Don Bosco, who tried every means to break down the wall of defiance behind which Albert had entrenched himself.

One day they met face to face on the stairs. There was no means of escape.

"Why do you avoid me like this, Albert?" asked Don Bosco gently. "You know you have

need of Confession, and as soon as possible."
The boy was silent.

"You won't? Well, listen to me. The time will
come when you will want me and will not find
me." One evening a little later, after night prayers,
Don Bosco said solemnly, "There is one here
among you who will be dead before the month
is over. He will not come to me, but I will recommend him to his Guardian Angel. The Feast
of the Immaculate Conception is coming near,
then Christmas, days to be approached with a
clean heart. Let him cleanse his own, for time
presses."

Albert, who seemed quite unmoved, avoided
Don Bosco more determinedly than ever and,
influenced by his friend, refused to go to Confession for either feast. On the 30th of December, rather against his will, Don Bosco was
induced by the Duchess of Montmorency-Laval,
his friend and benefactor, to preach the Forty
Hours devotions in the parish church of her
estate at Borgo.

"No one in the infirmary?" he asked before
he left. "I shall be away for four days."

"No one, you need have no anxiety."

That very evening, Albert was spoken to
severely by one of his old class companions, now
a seminarian.

"Look here, Albert," he said, "are you alive

or dead?"

"Dead," said Albert sharply, amidst the laughter of his companions.

There were hot cakes for supper, of which he ate so greedily that in the evening he was very ill. Peritonitis set in, and the doctor, hastily sent for, advised the last Sacraments.

"I want Don Bosco, I want Don Bosco!" wailed the boy. "I would not go to him, and now it is too late." Don Rua was there, and to him the boy made his Confession.

"Tell Don Bosco that I am very sorry," he said; "I don't deserve his forgiveness, but I know he will forgive me." Then, pointing to the boy who had been the cause of all his troubles, "Come here, Felix," he said; "you know it is your fault that I became estranged from Don Bosco, but I forgive you, as I hope God will forgive me."

Another big lad, held back by shame, would not make his general Confession. Don Bosco met him one day in a corridor.

"My boy," said the priest, "go to Confession to anyone you like. The main point is to make a good Confession. Go back to such-and-such a year and don't forget to mention this-and-that and that."

Flushed with confusion, the boy replied, "I will confess to you, Don Bosco, and now, this very minute."

Another day, passing by another boy, he whispered, "When are you going to make that general Confession? You need it badly."

"Why, I made it yesterday," said the boy, "to Father Piero."

"No, no," said Don Bosco, "you made a bad Confession; you did not tell him this," and he mentioned a sin that the penitent had been ashamed to speak of. The boy stared at him in stupefaction and burst into tears.

In the early days of the Oratory, a big boy, just admitted, who had a good deal on his conscience, determined to go to Confession at the church of the Consolata in the city before going to the Oratory to begin his new life. In the evening, he saw a group of boys gathered around Don Bosco and joined them. They were speaking of his wonderful power of reading souls, and several gave personal instances.

"Oh," said the newcomer, "I defy Don Bosco to read my soul. If he can, he is welcome to publish all my secrets."

"Come here," said the Saint, smiling, and bending down, he began to whisper in the boy's ear. Then, stopping, he looked steadily at him for a moment, and then began again. The boy got redder and redder.

"It was you, then," he burst out angrily, "who

heard my Confession at the Consolata today?"

The boys were all laughing. "What an idea!" they cried. "Besides, Don Bosco has not set foot outside the Oratory today."

A friend of Don Bosco's, on holiday at Nice, was speaking one day of this wonderful gift of his. There were some smiles of incredulity, and a certain lady remarked that she would very much like to put it to the test.

"If this worthy priest would undertake to tell me the state of my conscience," she said, "I might believe it."

It was unanimously decided to try it, and the lady wrote to him. She got her answer by return mail. "Be reconciled to your husband, and go back in your Confessions to such-and-such a year"—it was a matter of 20—"then you can set your mind at rest."

Not only had Don Bosco the gift of reading hearts. He was also, like several other saints, aware of an intolerable odor in those who had been guilty of any kind of impurity. These gifts of his were so well known that it sometimes happened that penitents, ashamed or lacking in courage to make a clean breast of it, would say to him, "Tell me my sins," and he would do so, while the penitent nodded acquiescence.

Sometimes the offer came from him. "Will you tell me or shall I tell you?" Sometimes before a great feast when he was assailed by crowds and there was not time to hear them all, he would go about among them: "You may go to Communion—and you—and you," he would say, touching a boy here and there, and then devote himself to the rest. It happened to him quite often to be eight or ten hours in the confessional. He would come out at 10 or 11 o'clock, faint with hunger, to sit down to a meal that had been waiting for three hours. It might happen even that he would find the refectory locked for the night and the cook, having forgotten all about him, gone to bed. Then he would smile; "A little break in the day's monotony," he would say. "I shall have a better appetite tomorrow."

He never would allow that he was tired. One night, after ten hours of it, two of his priests were on the way with him to his room when a young apprentice arrived and asked to go to Confession. Don Bosco was staggering with weariness, and the two looked at each other in dismay.

"Let him go, he can come back tomorrow," they both urged, but Don Bosco turned to the boy with a welcoming smile. "Come along, my son," he said, "I will hear you in my room."

It was the same always. At any hour of the day or night, he was always ready. Who was to know if the good moment, if put off, might ever come back? One St. Stephen's Day (December 26), after the long midnight Masses and the interminable Confessions that had preceded them, he was utterly worn out, when five or six of his Sunday boys arrived and asked him to hear them. He took them to his room, heard the Confessions of two and fell asleep on the shoulder of the third. The first two went away on tip-toe, the three who were waiting sat down very quietly, and the sixth knelt motionless beside his Father. A quarter of an hour later, Don Bosco awoke.

"My poor little fellow," he groaned, "how long have you been waiting? Why on earth did you not awaken me?"

"It would have been a sin, Father," they said; "you were so tired and you were sleeping so soundly."

"I shall never have such a chance again," said the little penitent proudly. "His head was on my shoulder all the time."

One day, they came to get Don Bosco to see two notable men of the day whom he had met in Rome and invited to come to see him if they happened to be in Turin. He was hearing the Confessions of his boys. "Please beg these gentlemen to wait," he said. "I cannot come now." Half an hour went by, an hour, an hour and a half—no Don Bosco! At last, with the departure of the last penitent, he was free.

"Don't be angry with me," he pleaded. "Some birds, you know, can only be had on the wing. Once you let them go, you may never catch them again."

He was inimitably patient. A boy might come back two or three times a day—to be received with the same kindness. "He had the gift above all others," said Cardinal Cagliero, one of his first boys, "of awakening in our hearts the most complete confidence in the mercy of God and the salutary fear of His justice. He was never surprised at relapses. 'Human nature is weak,' he would say, 'and the devil is always most active after a conversion. We can never have too much pity for those who have fallen.'"

The miracles of Don Bosco have remained famous. He was indignant when they were attributed to him. "I only tell people to invoke Our Lady," he would say; "it is all her doing." When very hard pressed, and by obvious facts, he would sometimes admit: "Well, you see, we work together, she and I."

On the day following the consecration of the great church of Our Lady, Help of Christians, a poor paralyzed woman insisted on being taken there in a cart. The crowd outside the building was so dense that the driver tried in vain to get through. At that moment, the sick woman caught sight of Don Bosco surrounded by people asking his blessing; jumping up, she walked toward him. "I am cured! I am cured!" she cried. "We can see that," said her friends, and escorted by the crowd, she went into the church to make a fervent thanksgiving.

Another day it was a blind girl who, led by two women, went to the church to pray and afterwards asked to see Don Bosco. "How long have you been blind?" he asked.

"My eyes have been bad for some time, but a year ago I went completely blind," she answered. "The doctors say it is hopeless," and she began to cry. Don Bosco led her to a window.

"Do you see light?" he asked.

"Nothing at all."

"Do you wish to see?"

"How can you ask such a question? I am a poor girl and my life depends on it."

"If you had your sight, would you use it for the good of your soul and for God's service?"

"Indeed I would!"

"Trust in Our Lady and she will help you."

"I know she will, but in the meantime I am blind."

Don Bosco held a medal of Our Lady before the sightless eyes. "What is this?" he said.

"I can see!" cried the girl; "it is a medal."

"Whose medal?"

"Our Lady's."

"And on this other side, what do you see?"

"An old man with a staff—oh, St. Joseph!"

"Holy Mother of God!" cried the two women. "She can actually see!"

The girl dropped the medal, which rolled into a dark corner of the room. One of them made a dash to recover it.

"Leave it alone," said Don Bosco; "let us see if Our Lady has really given her back her sight."

The girl went straight to the corner and picked up the medal. She was beside herself with joy. Later on she became a nun in the religious order founded by Don Bosco to do for girls what he himself was doing for boys.

A well-known doctor of Turin asked one day to speak to Don Bosco.

"I am told you cure all sorts of diseases."

"I? Not a bit of it."

"But I have been assured that it is true; I have been told of definite instances."

"Many people come here, you know, to pray to Our Lady, Help of Christians. If, after prayers and novenas, they obtain a cure, I have nothing to do with it; it is the work of Our Lady."

"Well, let her cure me, and I shall believe in miracles."

"What is the matter with you?"

The doctor had epilepsy, he said, and during

the past year the attacks had been so frequent that he could not go out unattended. In desperation he had come, like so many others, to Valdocco to beg for help.

"Well," said Don Bosco, "do like the others; kneel down with me and pray, and then cleanse your soul by Confession and Communion, and the Blessed Virgin will come to your aid."

"Ask me something else, I can't do that."

"Why not?"

"It would be hypocrisy. I don't believe in God, nor in the Blessed Virgin, nor in prayer, nor in miracles."

Don Bosco, greatly distressed, spoke to him with such burning and convincing fervor that the man ended by kneeling down and making the Sign of the Cross. "It is 40 years since I did that," he said. "I thought I had forgotten how." He ended by making an act of faith and receiving the Sacraments. The epilepsy vanished, never to return, and the doctor became a regular visitor at the church of Our Lady, who had cured him, both soul and body.

A certain general, dangerously ill, sent for Don Bosco, who heard his Confession but refrained from giving him the last Sacraments.

"The day after tomorrow," he said as he bade farewell to the invalid, "is the Feast of Our Lady, Help of Christians; pray to her, and in gratitude for your recovery, come to Holy Communion in her church."

The following day the general was a good deal worse, the danger was imminent, but the family had promised Don Bosco that the last Sacraments should not be given in his absence. At 8 o'clock that night, they went to tell Don Bosco that the doctors did not expect the sick man to live till morning. It was the eve of the great feast, and Don Bosco was busy hearing the Confessions of his boys.

"I cannot come now," he said. "I cannot send away all these children; I will come as soon as I can."

It was 11 before he was able to get away. A carriage was waiting for him at the door.

"Quick!" they said. "You will just be in time."

"Oh, people of little faith," he said, "did I not tell you that the general would receive Communion tomorrow on Our Lady's feast? It is nearly midnight and I have had no supper."

"Come, come, you can have it with us," they said as they drove off.

After supper, Don Bosco demanded to be driven back to the Oratory without visiting the invalid. He was lying so motionless that they thought he was dead. As a matter of fact, he was soundly and wholesomely asleep. The next morning, to everyone's profound amazement, he asked for his clothes. He intended, he said, to receive Communion from the hands of Don Bosco. The latter was vesting for Mass at about 8 o'clock when a rather pale individual appeared in the doorway.

"Here I am," he said.

"Ah, blessed be Our Lady, Help of Christians!" exclaimed Don Bosco. "Did I not tell you that you would be in her church on her feast day?"

Another day, a poor mother brought him her little crippled son, eight years old, on crutches, imploring him to do something. Don Bosco prayed to Our Lady, blessed the little fellow and gave him a medal—whereupon the child, throwing down his crutches, began to dance about the room. This was in Marseilles, where a new work had been originated but had been slow in taking hold. The rumor of the miracle gave it just the needed impetus. When asked what prayers he had said, Don Bosco answered, "Let us make a start, most Blessed Mother."

Another little boy of five, deaf and mute and unable to walk, was brought to Don Bosco in Turin. His parents had taken him to Rome, hoping that the Pope's blessing might work the desired miracle, but Pius IX only said: "Take the child to Don Bosco at Turin and see what he will do." At the sight of the poor little creature, the Saint, moved with pity, blessed him and began to pray. Then, taking him by the hand, he tried to coax him to walk. The child put out first one little leg and then the other, stood up and, holding Don Bosco's hand began to trot beside him. Don Bosco now got behind the child and sharply clapped his hands. The little fellow turned at the sound.

"He hears it, he hears it!" cried the parents, wild with joy.

"Now," said the Saint gently to the boy, "say after me, 'Daddy, Mommy.'" And for the first time the parents heard the words from the lips of their little son. Weeping with joy, they led him to the church of Our Lady to return thanks for the miracle obtained through her intercession. "We do things together," the Saint had said.

A new boy at the Oratory, Francis Dalmazzo, whose parents were better off than most of the others, found things rather harder than he had been accustomed to and hated the regular life. After a month of it, he wrote to his mother asking her to come and take him home as he could stand it no longer. On the day she arrived, her son, who wanted to go to Confession once more to Don Bosco before he left, joined the crowd who were waiting their turn before Mass. Presently an older boy, who helped in the refectory, came up to Don Bosco.

"There is no bread for breakfast," he said.

"Impossible," said Don Bosco. "Go to Father X . . . he will see about it."

A few minutes later the boy came back again, breathless. "We have searched everywhere. There are only a few rolls."

"Go to the baker, then, and get some more."

"He won't give us any more till his bill is paid—we owe him so much already."

"Very well, put what you can find in the basket, and God will see to it. I'll come presently and give it out."

Young Dalmazzo, who had overheard the whole conversation, was greatly interested. He had heard something of the wonders worked by Don Bosco and, following the boy to the refectory, took a good look at the basket. There were 15 rolls in it, and 300 hungry boys were waiting for their breakfast. At breakfast they came up, one by one—and each got a roll. Dalmazzo's eyes were starting out of his head. Don Bosco, with a smile and a kind word for each, went on with the distribution till the last of the 300 had passed. Dalmazzo flew to the basket and counted again. Just 15! He went straight to his mother. "I'm not going," he said; "I am never going." And he kept his word. He became a Salesian priest.

A still more wonderful thing happened on

Our Lady's birthday, when there were about 500 boys for Communion. The Ciborium was nearly empty. The sacristan had noticed it and had prepared a second one for consecration. But he forgot it, and it was not until after the Consecration of the Mass that, with a sudden gasp, he remembered that he had left it on the sacristy table. Don Bosco will be terribly distressed, he thought, and he won't be pleased with me. When at the moment of Communion the Saint uncovered the Ciborium, his dismay was evident. Clasping his hands, he looked upward in one tense moment of prayer, and then went down to the altar rail to give Communion to the kneeling line. The line arose and was succeeded by another, and then another. The Communions went on until the whole 500 had passed. When Don Bosco went back to the altar there was still one Host in the Ciborium. The sacristan was an astonished man.

A great source of joy for the boys at the Oratory was the moment when Don Bosco finished his supper, which he took together with his priests. He was generally late, and on that account was obliged to stay a little longer than the rest. The boys, who knew this, were on guard at the door, and the moment the others came out, they burst in. The room was packed; the first comers, of course, were the nearest, as close to their

Father as they could get. Some leaned on the back of his chair, others sat on the table, others on the floor, others knelt and others stood.

It looked as if there could be no possibility of reaching him. But there was. The smallest ones crawled in under the table on all fours, and little heads began popping up all around him. They were completely happy, for they had him all to themselves. But there was no want of respect in their devotion. He had only to raise a hand, and the whole room was in silence, listening, breathless, to a thrilling story, an amusing anecdote, or to some of those delightful questions that were always interesting and always made one think.

The charm of his presence kept them there, while the moments flew quickly past till it was time for evening prayers. "Let us try to make these little fellows know and love God," Don Bosco would often say. It might have been said of him that he showed them the beauty of God—in His servants. "There is a certain room at the Oratory," said a businessman in Turin, "where strange things happen—where every boy or young man who goes in with a heavy heart comes out radiant with joy. It is the room of Don Bosco."

And what about results? We are in a fallen world and there are always disappointments. Don Bosco knew it only too well. Yet he himself said

after many years of experience, "We succeed in
90 out of 100. And even in those with whom
we seem to have failed, there always remains
something—they are less dangerous."

Crispi, Freemason and anti-clerical, who for
so long was paramount in Italian politics, once
proposed to Don Bosco that he and his young
priests should take over the prison of Turin. On
certain conditions, said Don Bosco, he would
agree: complete liberty in religious matters, the
dismissal of all the guards, full governing powers and a daily allowance for the prisoners. The
agreement was ready and only waiting for the
minister's signature, when he suddenly refused.
"I know Don Bosco," he said; "he is capable of
turning all these convicts into priests, and we
have too many already."

The prisons were always for Don Bosco a
fruitful field of apostolate. He had the gift of
touching the most hardened hearts, and when
the last moments approached, he was unwearying in his care. Once in his student days, when
Don Cafasso, to prepare them for hearing Confessions, made his young clerics act to each other
the part of penitents, Don Bosco was told to
present himself as a little street urchin. He did
it perfectly, but the young companion who was
acting the part of confessor seemed a little shocked
at his avowals and became rather stern. Don

Bosco refused to say another word, hanging his head in silence.

"You've gone to work the wrong way altogether," said Don Cafasso; "you have frightened the poor little fellow." He turned to the pretended penitent. "Come, my son," he said, "have you nothing more to tell me? Don't be afraid. Perhaps it was this—or that."

"Yes, Father," said Don Bosco, looking up again. "I am not afraid to tell you all about it, but that priest made me so ashamed that I would never have dared to go on."

Even in those days he was a good judge of human nature.

Chapter 7

"ASK AND YOU SHALL RECEIVE"

ST. JOHN BOSCO'S life was one long prayer. He asked for souls—all the rest was only the means to that end. He asked for buildings to house his boys, for churches, he asked for priests to help him in the work—they came. When his enterprises became too much for him alone, he turned to the Catholic laymen—and women—of Turin. "There is work for you all," he said, "for every taste and every talent. You are the spoiled children of God will you not come to His help in the persons of my poor little outcasts?" And they came too from every rank of society, to do anything that was given them to do.

Men offered themselves for night classes, to look up the young workers at the factories, to organize plays for them, to visit them in their homes and to try to get them work. Women made clothes for them, mended what could be mended, washed and cleaned what might still be useful, taught them how to keep themselves clean, washed and combed the little ones until, when they went to ask for work, they were presentable and had a chance of getting it. The great army of Salesian Cooperators was coming into existence.

Without a penny in his pocket, Don Bosco built houses, churches, workshops; he fed and taught hundreds of children, educated priests— and somehow the money always came. Indeed, this was not without care and anxiety, not without heart-breaking moments that tested a faith and confidence that was always to be—as the greatest surely must be—fire-tried.

Once when Don Bosco was in Rome, Pope Pius IX, in token of appreciation of his splendid work, wanted to make him a Monsignor.

"Oh, Holy Father, I beseech you!" he cried. "A nice figure I should be in purple among my little ragged boys! They would hardly recognize me, and I should lose their confidence completely. And then, think of all the kind people who help me so generously—they would think I was rich, and I should not have the face to go begging. Please do not think of such a thing, please leave me to be 'poor Don Bosco.'" The Pope, who was all his life Don Bosco's firm friend, accepted his plea and honored him in other ways, by advice, by kindness and by generous gifts. Once when he was taking leave of him, the Pope put a sum of money into his hands. "There, Don Bosco," he said, "that is for a great feast for your boys when you get home."

He was in Rome once more at the time of the Conclave which was to elect Pius IX's successor, and in a corridor of the Vatican he met Cardinal Pecci face to face. He looked at him fixedly for a moment and then knelt. "May I kiss Your Eminence's hand?" he asked.

"Who are you?" asked the Cardinal.

"I am a poor priest," said Don Bosco, "who wants to kiss your hand before—in a few days . . . I hope to kiss your feet."

"I forbid you to pray for anything of the kind," said Cardinal Pecci.

"You can't forbid me to pray for God's Will," said Don Bosco.

"If you are not careful," said the Cardinal, "I will have you suspended."

"Oh, Your Eminence, you can't do that at present. When you can, I will be all submission."

"But who are you, to go on like that?"

"I am Don Bosco."

"Be quiet," said the Cardinal, "it is not the time for joking but for work," and he went on his way.

A week later he was being proclaimed as Pope Leo XIII.

After the simple cordiality and keen sense of humor of Pius IX, Don Bosco found the new Pope very dignified and rather cold. But Leo XIII had other ways of winning hearts, and Don Bosco's first audience ended in a happy certainty that he had as strong a friend in the new Pope as in the old.

Help came to him sometimes in strange ways. An irate builder arrived one day demanding payment. Don Rua, the bursar, whose cash box was, as usual, empty, tried to put him off, but the man began to bluster and shout: "This won't do. I insist on seeing Don Bosco." He was taken to a room next to the Saint's where several people were already waiting and sat down, angry and growling.

Presently in walked an imperious gentleman who asked shortly to see Don Bosco.

"I must see him at once," he declared.

"Will you kindly sit down and wait your turn?" he was asked.

"I have no time to wait," he replied sharply and, striding straight over to Don Bosco's door, rapped on it loudly. A visitor was inside. Don Bosco appeared in the doorway.

"What can I do for you?" he asked.

"I want to speak to you."

"Would you mind waiting a few minutes?"

"I have no time to wait," said the stranger,

and without more ado walked straight in. Though his behavior was not very reassuring, Don Bosco asked him to sit down.

"I do not want to sit down. Here, take this," and he planted a small parcel on the table.

"Good-bye, Father, pray for me," he said, and marched out as quickly as he had come in.

A friendly Countess was next on the waiting list. "I hope you are all right, Father," she said. "I didn't like the look of that man at all. I hope he has not done you any harm."

"Not much harm," said Don Bosco, smiling. And he opened out a bundle of bills for exactly the amount that was owing to the angry trades-man. These were duly presented to him when he came in blustering a little later. He was rather taken aback and began to excuse himself. "They told me you couldn't pay me," he said. "I ought not to have believed them."

Another day, there was a considerable sum to be paid for taxes. The utmost limit of delay had been reached and there was a threat of legal pro-ceedings. Don Rua, at his wits' end, went off to find Don Bosco. "I haven't a cent," he said. "Let us pray to Our Lady," answered the Saint, and he went on quietly with his work. Presently there was a knock at the door. A gentleman was asking for Don Bosco. "Father," he said, "I am not a rich man, but I had this little sum put by and I should like you to have it." It was exactly what was needed for the taxes.

On another occasion, Don Rua was being pressed for payment by the baker, who flatly refused to give any more credit. Count A . . . , who had arrived at the critical moment to beg prayers for his wife who was ill, gave half of what was needed. Don Bosco set all his boys to praying, and a few days later the same amount was sent again by the grateful Count, whose wife had completely recovered.

At the time of the planning of the Church of Our Lady, Help of Christians, Don Bosco paid a visit to the city of Nice, where in the company of several friends he examined the plans of the architect.

"It is beautiful," he said, "but the foundations alone will cost 30,000 dollars."

"I am afraid you won't be able to collect that sum in Nice," said a gentleman who was present. "We have had so many calls this winter."

"But I need it," said Don Bosco, "and at once."

After lunch that day, a lawyer arose and came up to him. "I have to inform you, Don Bosco," he said, "that a client of mine has just given me 30,000 dollars for you. You have only to come to my office whenever you want it."

"Blessed be Our Lady, Help of Christians!"

cried Don Bosco in deep thanksgiving.

It happened again, as so often before, that Don Rua had a bill to pay and had nothing to pay it with. It was not a very large one, but everything is large when you have not the wherewithal to pay. Don Bosco, who was going away the next day, was busy. "Do your best," he said in answer to Don Rua's anxious appeal. Every available resource was explored, but in vain.

"We are still short of some 30 dollars," groaned Don Rua, "and if they don't have it tomorrow they will sue us. You surely won't go away and leave us in such straits!"

"But what can I do?" said Don Bosco. He did as usual—he had recourse to Heaven. The next morning Don Rua was making one last frantic appeal to his chief when a friend of Don Bosco's came to ask for an interview.

"I'm so sorry," said Don Bosco, "but I am just off to catch a train."

"But it's about some money."

"Give it to Don Rua and come with me. We can talk on the way to the station."

This man was one of the greatest benefactors of the Society, who used to bring an offering every week. As they went off together, he told Don Bosco that that very morning he had been moved to come and pay for a few lottery tickets he had asked him for. He resisted the idea at first, since it was not his day for coming, but it had obsessed him so tormentingly that he had ended by coming.

"What was the price of what you asked for?"

"Oh, not very much, 30 dollars or so."

Don Bosco laughed. "And you would have let me miss my train for that?" he said. "Go back to Don Rua and he will tell you all about it. We won't be sued, not this time anyhow."

"Whenever he had a penny, he spent two," said an old friend, "and he never had a moment's doubt. He went straight on, quietly and calmly, unconquerable in steadfastness and hope, and he invariably attained his end. Having nothing, he obtained all things, and however wild his projects seemed in the eyes of the world, in the end they were accomplished. It is true that he did not spare himself. His days were crushing, his nights reduced till there was very little left. When his sons begged him to take a rest—'in Heaven,' he said, 'not on earth. When the devil rests in his work of ruining souls, then will I rest from fighting for them.'"

To a lady who asked him for a good investment for her fortune, he opened out both his hands.

"I won't let you go," said another lady, also very wealthy, "till you have given me your autograph." On a piece of paper he wrote: "Received from Madam X . . ., the sum of 2,000 dollars for my works—John Bosco," and offered it with a smile.

A humble benefactor of the Oratory was Joseph Bosco, the Saint's older brother. Whenever he came to Turin, he paid a visit to Valdocco; and when Don Bosco took, as he often did, a party of boys to Becchi for a few days' holiday, Joseph would spare himself no inconvenience to make them comfortable and happy. One day, when he came to Turin with the intention of buying two calves, he found his brother in great straits for money.

"Take this," he said, offering him all he had. "I was going to spend it at the market, but you need it far more than I do."

"But what about your calves?" asked Don Bosco.

"They can wait till another time."

"I will pay it back," said Don Bosco, "as soon as I have a little money."

"No, no, you never have any to spare," said Joseph. "It is a gift; I have all I want."

One day some time after, Joseph arrived rather unexpectedly. He had some debts to settle, he said, and wanted to go to Confession.

"I've had a sort of warning not to put it off."

"Stay with us for a few days," said Don Bosco, but he could not persuade him. In a short time, however, he was back again.

"Anything wrong at home?" asked Don Bosco, surprised.

"No, but I want your advice. I have made myself surety for the debts of someone. If I live, it will be all right, but what if I die?"

"Why, in that case, he will have to pay."

"I should not like my friend to be at a loss after I had given my word."

"Well," said Don Bosco, "if that is worrying you, I will be guarantee."

"I am so grateful—now my mind is at rest," said Joseph.

He went home, settled his affairs as if he were preparing for death, and a few weeks later he fell ill. Don Bosco arrived in time to comfort his last moments, and Joseph died in his arms.

On his first visit to Florence, to beg pledges for his work, Don Bosco was invited to meet some ladies and gentlemen of the town.

"Why are you going back so soon?" they asked. "Could you not stay a few days?"

"My boys are waiting for me," he answered.

"Let them wait, it won't hurt them for a few days. What does it matter?"

"It matters a good deal," said Don Bosco; "they will have nothing to eat. Who will give them their daily bread if I stay here?"

"If you were to stay for a few days, how much

would it take to feed your boys?"

He named a sum.

"If we find that sum will you stay?"

"Yes, there is nothing to prevent it."

"Very well, you shall have it, it shall be sent to the Archbishop's house tonight."

"How on earth do you manage to keep all those enterprises of yours going?" a politician once asked him. "It is a mystery to me."

"I go on like a steam engine," said Don Bosco.

"Yes, but how do you keep the engine going?"

"One needs fire, and something to feed the fire."

"What do you mean by that?" asked the man.

"The fire of faith and confidence in God," said Don Bosco, "for without it empires and kingdoms fall and the work of man is useless."

The words and the tone in which they were spoken made a profound impression on the listener.

Until the work of his own foundations became too tremendous, Don Bosco was at the service of all the clergy of Piedmont. Novenas, triduums, jubilees, panegyrics, retreats, missions—the requests were endless, and to the best of his ability he complied with them all. In our days of easy traveling, it is difficult to imagine the weariness of this continual journeying. A rumbling old coach, freezing in winter and stifling in sum-

mer, was the only means of locomotion for those
who, like Don Bosco, could not pay for a comfortable traveling carriage. And once he got there,
it was no great eloquence—a friendly, fatherly
talk, a grave and gentle insistence on the great
truths of religion, and behind it all the most
powerful thing in the world—a man of prayer.
No wonder that his preaching was like a wind
of the Spirit blowing through the souls of men,
wakening them to a sudden understanding, however elementary, of the things of eternity. His
mother was his most valued critic. In the early
days, he would read his sermons to her and be
guided by her sure judgment. He would rewrite
a passage if she disapproved.

"What on earth do you mean by that, John?"
she asked one day when he had used a rather
abstruse word to describe the office of St. Peter.

"It means door-keeper, Mother," he said.

"Then why don't you say door-keeper? People would understand what you mean."

He was very fond of a simulated conversation
in his sermons. It woke people up and made
them think.

Among all the strange episodes in the life of
Don Bosco, one of the strangest was the appearance of the dog "Grigio"—a huge grey hound
that appeared suddenly at a moment of danger,
reappeared on many occasions and disappeared

some years later when the danger was over. He asked for neither food nor shelter, was savage as a wolf against an enemy, but gentle as a lamb with the boys of the Oratory, who gave him the name of Grigio—"the grey one."

Don Bosco was once passing through the thickly populated quarter which lay near Valdocco late at night. It had a bad reputation: shady characters could skulk behind the tufts of scrub and brushwood and burst out upon the passerby. Margaret Bosco was always anxious when her son was out late at night. Don Bosco had passed the last buildings of the town when a huge grey dog appeared and walked by his side.

He was startled at first, but as he found that the creature seemed friendly, he accepted its company and went on to the Oratory. When he reached the door the dog turned around and trotted off in the direction whence it had come. Every night henceforward, when Don Bosco was out late, the same thing happened. He found the dog waiting for him whenever there was a lonely part of the town to be traversed.

One night, he became aware of two suspicious-looking men who were following him, matching their pace to his. When he tried to avoid them by crossing the road, they crossed too. He decided to turn back, but at the moment he did so they were on him. A cloak was thrown over his head and a handkerchief thrust into his mouth. He struggled to free himself and call for help, but it was useless. Suddenly, with a terrific howl, Grigio appeared and rushed upon them. Leaping on the one who held the cloak, he forced him to let go, then bit the second and flung him onto the ground. The first tried to escape but Grigio was after him, rolled him too in the mud and stood over them both, growling furiously.

"Call off your dog!" they cried to Don Bosco.

"I will call him off if you will let me go about my business," he replied.

"Anything you like, only call him off!"

"Come, Grigio," said Don Bosco, and the dog immediately obeyed, while the two men made off in double quick time.

Another night, he was on his way home when a man hiding behind a tree fired twice at him, at such close range that there would have been short shrift for him had not both shots missed. Then, throwing away the pistol, the man rushed upon him. But at this moment Grigio appeared again, seized the man and dragged him off. He fled in terror, and the dog once more escorted Don Bosco home.

On another occasion it was from a whole band that this mysterious companion saved him. He had reached a lonely spot when, hearing steps, he turned to see a man close to him with an uplifted stick. Don Bosco was a swift runner in those days, but his enemy was swifter and soon caught up with him. It was a moment of action. Don Bosco, with a well-directed blow of the fist, sent the man sprawling. His howl of pain brought several others out of the bushes where they had been hiding. They were all armed with heavy sticks, and things looked black for Don Bosco. Once more, at the crucial moment, the terrific howl of Grigio was heard. He ran around and around his master, growling and showing his formidable teeth until one by one the ruffians dropped off and disappeared.

One night, instead of accompanying Don Bosco, Grigio went to the Oratory and refused to let him go out, lying down across the door of his room, for once growling and showing illtemper when he made the slightest attempt to dislodge him.

"Don't go out, John," said his mother; "if you won't listen to me, at least listen to that dog; he has more sense than you have."

Don Bosco gave in at last, and a quarter of an hour later a neighbor came in to warn him that he had overheard two rogues planning to attack him.

Another evening after supper the dog appeared

in the playroom, and all the boys gathered around him and made much of him. They patted him, pulled his ears, stroked his head, the little ones rode on him. He regarded them with grave eyes until at last they brought him into the refectory where Don Bosco was still at supper. "Why, Grigio, old fellow, what brings you here?" said he. Grigio went up to him, put his great head on the table, looked at him and wagged his tail.

"What do you want, old boy? A bit of cheese or polenta?" No, he wanted neither. "Then, if you won't have anything," said his master, stroking the great head, "go home to bed." Grigio gave him one long look, turned around and solemnly trotted out. The reason of this unusual visit suddenly dawned on them. Don Bosco had been spending the evening with his kind friend the Marquis Fassati. In the ordinary course of affairs he would have walked back alone, but that night his friend had induced him to let him drive him home in his carriage. Grigio, waiting in one of his dark corners, had missed him and, anxious about his safety, had come to see if he was at home.

The last time Don Bosco saw him was one night in Castelnuovo. He was going from Murialdo to Moncucco and it was growing dark. He had to pass some farms and vineyards that were guarded by savage dogs. "I wish I had Grigio here," he said to himself. As if the wish had suddenly produced him, Grigio appeared with every sign of delight at meeting his friend and walked the whole way with him. It was lucky he was there, for two fierce dogs at a farm they passed rushed out upon them, but Grigio soon sent them flying with their tails between their legs. When Don Bosco reached the friend's house to which he was bound, they were astonished to see the magnificent dog and wondered where Don Bosco had picked him up. When they sat down to supper he was lying beside them, but when Don Bosco rose to give him some food, he was not to be seen. That was the last of Grigio. The enemies of the Saint had grown tired of plotting against him.

By 1869, the Society had received Papal approbation, but the rules and constitutions of the Congregation had not yet been passed. Cardinals, archbishops and bishops in Rome had expressed their admiration for Don Bosco's work, but he had a powerful opponent at home. Monsignor Gastaldi, the new Archbishop of Turin, an able and fervent prelate but with very definite ideas of his own, though he had been a great friend of Don Bosco, was wholly out of sympathy with the newly founded Order. He was convinced that it was too unusual in its lines and too likely to draw vocations away from

the archdiocese. Unfavorable reports were so sed-
ulously circulated that they were bound to have
an effect in Rome. Don Bosco's discipline was
not sufficiently strong; the studies of his young
priests were neglected; his professors of theology were not well grounded; the novitiate scarcely
existed; the ascetic training of the young Salesians was incomplete; the fact that while teaching they were continuing their own studies was
harmful to both, and one or other of the two
was bound to suffer.

To meet this new danger, Don Bosco made
two more journeys to Rome. He printed a booklet refuting the most serious of the accusations
and distributed it among the most influential
people in Rome. He then ordered a triduum of
prayer in which priests, religious and boys were
to join to implore the help of Our Lady. On
the day when the question was discussed, Don
Bosco was at the house of the Secretary of the
Congregation awaiting his return from the meeting. "Light your lamps, Don Bosco," he called,
as he came in, "light your lamps! Your Rules are
finally approved." After 16 years of weariness,
labor and anxiety, the Salesian Congregation was
at last safely on its feet.

"If, knowing what I know now," said Don
Bosco later, "I had to begin over again all the
labor that the Society has cost me and endure

all the consequent suffering, I am not sure that I would have the courage to do it."

To relieve the pressure on the Oratory at Valdocco, Don Bosco had founded a second one, dedicated to St. Aloysius Gonzaga, at the other side of the town, where Don Borel, Don Murialdo and later Don Rua were working for the young people of that quarter. It was almost as sparsely populated as Valdocco when Don Bosco took possession, and equally poor. The neighborhood of the river made it the constant haunt of washerwomen, and young hooligans ready for any mischief were not wanting. The place and the people were waiting for Don Bosco.

Unfortunately, the Waldensians (a Protestant sect) also took a fancy to the locality, and soon after the founding of St. Aloysius', they made it their chief center. They built a large church, schools and workshops. It was a moment for action, and Don Bosco, who had only lately finished his great Church of Our Lady, Help of Christians, determined to build another. The Waldensians, however, got wind of the project, and as they had bought up a good deal of the surrounding land, they refused to sell. It was eight years before Don Bosco succeeded in getting what he wanted and a royal decree proclaiming the necessity of a church in that quarter.

The building was planned and the foundation stone was laid. Thanks to the generosity of friends the work went on apace, and in four years the church was finished and dedicated to St. John in honor of Pope Pius IX, whose name before ascending the Throne of Peter had been John Mastai-Ferretti. At the entrance of the church Don Bosco placed a large marble statue of the Pope. The church was his thank offering to the great Pontiff who had been so good a friend to him.

One might have thought that Don Bosco could now take a rest from church building, but it was not to be. A few months before the death of Pius IX, a project had been formed by the Catholics of Rome to build a great church dedicated to the Sacred Heart on the Esquiline Hill, and the Pope himself had bought the land for it. That part of Rome was growing rapidly. There were several Protestant chapels there, but no large Catholic church. Pope Leo XIII appealed to the Catholic world to help in the enterprise. The foundations were laid, but with great difficulty, since it was necessary to dig down 54 feet to escape the tunnels of some old porphyry mines, with the result that the whole of the available funds were exhausted. Leo XIII, discussing the matter one day with some of his cardinals, was full of regret at the sudden check.

"What can we do?" he asked.

"I only see one way out of it, Your Holiness," said Cardinal Alimonda.

"What is that?"

"Put Don Bosco in charge of it; he will do it."

"Would he undertake it?"

"I know him—the wish of the Pope will be enough for him."

The Pope acted on the advice. Don Bosco happened to be in Rome at that very moment on business connected with his missionary enterprises. He was invited to an audience, and this rather weighty honor was conferred on him. Back in Turin, he put it before his council, who protested strongly against this new burden, but he won them all over. It was finally decided to ask that beside the church there should be a large home for the poor and homeless boys of Rome. Then the Saint began to collect. Circulars were addressed to the whole Catholic world, lotteries were set in motion; the aristocracy of Rome gave the 12 great granite columns on which the church was to rest, Catholic Italy gave the facade of the building.

"Is it moving along?" asked the Pope one day of Don Bosco.

"It is moving along grandly," was the reply, "but it is beginning to weigh rather heavily on my poor old shoulders."

"Take this," said the Pope, giving him a roll

of 5,000 dollars; "it has just been given to me."

But 5,000 dollars did not go very far, and the work was soon at a standstill for lack of funds. Don Bosco decided to go to France. There had been an attempt to found an Oratory on the lines of Valdocco at Nice, and he had been often begged to come and see about it. They took him straight to a fine property that was for sale. He went over it hastily.

"It will do for us very well," he said.

"No doubt," said the lawyer who accompanied him, "but it might be as well to look at something cheaper. They want 90,000 dollars for this, and you do not have enough to pay the contract."

"True," said Don Bosco, "I have nothing, but I have an idea that when all expenses are paid, we shall have some 12,000 dollars left over."

The lawyer, who did not know Don Bosco's little ways, gazed at him in amazement, wondering whether his companion was the kind of man it was safe to let walk about alone.

But Don Bosco's confidence was catching.

Msgr. Mermillod preached a magnificent sermon in favor of the work—so magnificent, learned and eloquent that Don Bosco, who was very tired, and whose knowledge of French was limited, slumbered peacefully till it was time for the collection, which amounted to 5,000 dollars. Gifts came pouring in so rapidly that when the property was bought and paid for, there remained 12,000 dollars to spare. The astonished lawyer reversed his decision. The people flocked to see Don Bosco; the general opinion was that he was a saint. He was invited to lunch and to dinner with all the notables of the place, and—since they had opened their purses to him as well as their houses—he went.

"That is no saint," said a worthy lady to a friend—at a safe distance—seeing the holy man eat and drink like everybody else. As he left the house, she was on his passage.

"Madame," he remarked gently, turning in her direction, "do you remember the words of St. Paul, 'Whether you eat or drink or whatever you do, do it all for the glory of God'?" And as by no human possibility could he have heard her remark, she also reversed her decision.

That was the first of many visits to France. He was at Toulouse and Marseilles some years later, where he was so mobbed that it was decided that he should drive to a neighboring town and take the train there. The parish priest, who undertook to drive him, stopped at the house of one of his own parishioners, dangerously ill.

"There already?" asked Don Bosco.

"No," said the good priest, "but I want you to see someone here."

A young girl, the daughter of the house, had a disease of the throat which prevented her from swallowing, and she was dying of thirst.

"Drink a glass of water," said Don Bosco with authority.

"She can't," sobbed the mother.

"Then let us pray."

They prayed for a few moments, and Don Bosco arose.

"Drink it now," he said, and she drank it, crying, "I am cured!"

"Blessed be God and His holy Mother," murmured Don Bosco, and went on to the station.

His last journey was to Paris, and he took it by assault. Cardinal Guibert, the Archbishop, suggested that he should preach in the Madeleine in favor of his works.

"But, Your Eminence, I speak French so badly!"

"Never mind," said the Cardinal, "Paris will understand."

And Paris did. In the pulpit where France's greatest orators had swayed breathless crowds, this shabby old country priest stood up and spoke. His French, as he had said, was bad, his accent worse; at times he stopped to consult a dictionary, and the people—that people who know what eloquence means—wept. Heart and soul spoke through the halting medium, and it was the heart and soul of a saint.

The great house where he was staying was besieged. People waited for hours for the chance of one word with him, touching his poor old cassock, of kissing the worn old hand that gave away medals of Our Lady. One day it was an assault. Even the street outside was full, and crowds were waiting on the staircase and land-ings. Suddenly, a homely old country priest made his appearance, trying to work his way through the crowd to the door of Don Bosco's room.

"Please don't push like that, Father," said the people who had been waiting for hours. "You must wait your turn like everybody else. Ask the secretary and he will give you a number. We want to see Don Bosco just as much as you do."

"But you won't see him unless you let me in," said the old priest. "I am Don Bosco."

"You Don Bosco! Do you think you are going to take in the people of Paris like that? Try your jokes on someone else!"

And Don Bosco, since they would not let him into his own room, turned quietly on his heel and went to visit a sick lady who had begged to see him but had had to be refused for lack of time.

When Don Bosco left France, he had enough money to feed all his children and to pay for the completion of the Church of the Sacred Heart in Rome.

Chapter 8

THE SAVING CROSS

IN THOSE early days of a united Italy, with a capital that had been snatched from the Pope, there was a strong hostility between Church and State, and Don Bosco's attitude toward the frequently hostile government provoked criticism. "My politics are those of the Our Father," he would reply—"Thy kingdom come." Hostile to the Church and to religion as the ministers of the new regime so often were, they had souls to be saved, and for Don Bosco to be friends with them would not only give them a chance of sharing in his good works but would give him a chance to use what influence he could to help them.

"If, in order to reach a soul, I had to take off my hat to the devil, I would do it at once," he said on one occasion.

"Today I have written to three important people," he said another day as he came into the refectory, a packet of letters in his hand—"to the King, the Pope and the hangman." There

155

was a general laugh. No one was surprised at the two latter—the Pope went without saying, and the hangman too, for Don Bosco was always in and out of the prisons. But the King . . . The law abolishing all the convents in Italy was about to be passed, and Don Bosco had had a strange dream of the impending death of the Queen and the Queen Mother. Believing it to be a warning from Heaven, he had written his dream to the King—who took no notice. The law was passed, and within two months the Queen, the Queen Mother and the Duke of Genoa, Victor Emmanuel's brother, were dead.

There were men among the new ministers to whom the fact of a letter to or from the Pope meant treason to the State and an incipient revolution. Rumors were circulated that the boys of the Oratory were being trained to war and that vast stores of ammunition were being accumulated for an uprising. Things came to a head when Farini, Minister of the Interior, issued a search warrant and a band of police went to the house. Some were placed on guard at the doors, others posted themselves at different points and watched every movement of the boys.

"Would you mind letting me see your warrant for this visit?" asked Don Bosco politely. "Otherwise I am afraid I cannot let you in."

"We'll see about that," retorted the visitors.

"You surely know that it is against the law to break into a private house like this," he replied, whereupon a man was sent in all haste to get the mandate. It accused Don Bosco, with four of his friends, of compromising correspondence with the exiled Jesuits, with Msgr. Franzoni, Archbishop of Turin, also in exile, and with the court of Rome. Taking him to his room, they proceeded to search him from head to foot with a rough disrespect that caused him to murmur gently to himself, "*Et cum iniquis reputatus est*" ("And with the wicked he was reputed"—*Mark* 15:28). "What's that?" queried the officer. "Only that you are doing me the same kind of service that certain people did to Our Lord," he replied. They went on to search through everything in the rooms, especially the waste-paper basket. Nothing. Tired and rather cross, they finally turned to him in disgust.

"Come," they said, "we are wasting our time, give up those papers."

"What papers?"

"The ones we want."

"I can't give you what I do not have."

"You have no papers proving your relations with the Jesuits, the Archbishop and the Pope?"

"No; do I look like a fool?"

"I can't say that you do."

"Then do you think that if I had such papers

I would be keeping them here, at a time like this? If you want to go on wasting your time it is your own affair; I have work to do," and he sat down and began to write letters. As soon as each one was finished they snatched it and examined it closely. Suddenly, while hunting through a big box, they found a locked compartment.

"What is this?" they cried triumphantly.

"It's a secret of mine," said Don Bosco gravely.

"Open it."

"I am sorry, I cannot. One has the right to hide documents that might bring discredit on oneself or on one's family. Please leave it alone."

"Open it, or we will break the lock."

He unlocked it, and they fell upon a bundle of papers which informed them that Don Bosco owed a large sum of money to his baker, another to a tanner who had furnished leather for the shoemaking, and several other smaller sums for oil, rice and macaroni. They looked foolish. Presently they discovered a collection of the works of the Bollandists.

"What are these books?"

"Oh, those are books written by the Jesuits."

"The Jesuits! Aha! We will confiscate them."

"Let us see what they're about first," said another, dismayed at the size of the collection.

"They are the Lives of the Saints, very edifying," said Don Bosco, and opening a volume, he began to read the life of St. Simeon Stylites.

"That will do, that's enough," said the visitors hastily—and the Bollandists were left in peace.

At 5 o'clock in the afternoon, Don Bosco reminded them that it was Pentecost Eve and that he had several hundred children waiting to go to Confession.

"Very well, we have finished," they said, "but how is it that, whereas our visits usually have the effect of frightening people, you seem rather to be amused?"

"My good men," he said, "I have a clear conscience."

The fact that in the end they could not help believing him did not prevent them from seizing his mail which arrived at that moment. The first letter was from a Cabinet Minister, begging him to take charge of a homeless orphan and sending a small offering for his keep. The signature was the very one which figured on their search warrant—human nature is inconsistent. In their astonishment they forgot the rest of the correspondence—just as well, perhaps, as there was a letter from Rome into which they would certainly have read all kinds of treason. They went off in a quite friendly fashion after a glass of wine, which Don Bosco was sure they must have needed after their long and arduous labors.

The danger seemed averted; but it was not so. Two weeks later the Oratory was visited again, and this time Don Bosco was out. The visitors were three in number—Farini's secretary, an Inspector of schools, and a professor from the university. Their aim was to discover the sources of Don Bosco's income and to find something compromising in the teaching. To force Don Alasonatti, the bursar, into acknowledging that the house was kept up by secret donations from the Pope and the exiled Italian princes, they plied him with such rude and bullying questions, and with such savage insults, that what with fear and anxiety, he fainted.

Don Bosco, coming in from a begging expedition in the town, found him in that condition and told the visitors freely and frankly what he thought of their behavior. Their close questioning elicited nothing from him but what they had already heard from the bursar: the house was supported by the meager pensions of a few of the boys, by the charity of friends and the long-suffering credit of the tradesmen. Beaten on that point, the inquisitors still hoped to be able to condemn the teaching. They visited every class, posing insidious questions—which were readily and intelligently answered by the boys.

"How many kinds of monarchical government are there?"

"Two: absolute and constitutional."

"Which is the best?"

"All forms of government are good if carried out by good men."

"Who killed Julius Caesar?"

"Brutus."

"Don't you think he was right to kill a tyrant?"

"No, for a subject should never revolt against his leader."

"But if the leader does harm?"

"Then God will punish him."

"Would it not be right to stimulate a rising against Victor Emmanuel to make him understand that he must leave the Pope and bishops and priests alone?"

"No, that would not be right. His subjects must pray and endure."

"But all persecutors of the Church are wicked. Victor Emmanuel persecutes the Church—therefore . . ."

"You know more about it than I do, Sir, and are better able to judge. Don Bosco always teaches us to respect the King and the royal family. People don't say that kind of thing here."

This was not encouraging. The visitors went to the kitchen, then to the refectory to see if they could not prove that the children were starved, then to the church and the workshops. Every cupboard, every tool chest was opened and searched. For seven hours the examination went on and only one item was discovered, a page of Latin from a well-known encyclical of Pius IX which had been used as an exercise in dictation. All the writing books of that class were confiscated; it might be proved to be a political offense.

"A clever man, that priest," they said as they took off. "No means of catching him, and how those boys do love him!"

Disgusted at finding nothing that could be brought against Don Bosco, his enemies proceeded to examine men who at different times had been employed by him. The first was a shoemaker who had taught in the workshop and who was also a doorkeeper. They questioned him as to Don Bosco's politics.

"His only politics are how to provide for his poor boys," was the answer.

"Does he not speak to you and others about joining the Pope's soldiers to make war on the King?"

"The only fighting he speaks about is fighting against the devil by means of prayer and the Sacraments."

"We hear that Pius IX has sent him a large sum of money."

"When he was last in Rome the Pope gave him some money for a feast for his boys. If he had given him more, Don Bosco would not have to be always begging and always in debt."

Don Bosco's old friend Rattazzi, who was no longer in the ministry, having heard of the visitations, sent for him and made him give a full account of all that had happened. He was very angry. "I don't love priests," he said, "but I admire good work, whoever does it." He suggested that the matter should be brought up in Parliament, but Don Bosco said he would rather write a private letter to the Minister of the Interior and the Minister of Public Instruction. For the rest, he would leave himself and his affairs in the hands of Providence. He wrote, as he had proposed, a full account of his work and his activities and a description of the visits to which he had been subjected.

He might have saved himself the trouble. Mischievous and calumniating attacks of the press continued to describe the Oratory as a nest of sedition, and the Ministers in office were quite ready to believe anything that was against a priest.

Things looked so black that Don Bosco at last determined to beard Farini in his den and try to make him listen to reason. Having applied for an audience and been refused, he wrote to Spaventa, Farini's secretary. He was put off day after day in the hope of wearing him out; but Don Bosco persisted, and at last hopes of an

audience were held out for 11 o'clock on a certain morning. Don Bosco went to the Minister's house and sent in his name. A message was
brought to him that, owing to pressing business,
he could not be received.

"I will wait till the Secretary is able to see
me," he said calmly and sat down. He waited,
fasting, till 6 o'clock in the evening. People of
every kind came and went. They seemed to have
no difficulty in getting in, and even the ushers
began to show a certain indignation. Spaventa,
perhaps aware of this feeling, came at last to the
door of his room.

"What do you want, Don Bosco?" he shouted
rudely.

"I want a few minutes' conversation with you,"
answered Don Bosco.

"What do you want?"

"My business is private."

"You can speak here; these people are trust-
worthy."

"Signore," said Don Bosco firmly, "I have 500
poor boys to maintain. I put them in your hands
and ask you to provide for their future."

"Who are these boys?"

"They are for the most part homeless orphans
whom the Government sent to me and now
seems inclined to turn out into the street."

"Where are they?"

"In my house."

"Who maintains them?"

"The charity of my friends."

"What does the Government pay for them?"

"Not one cent."

During this conversation the people in the antechamber, greatly interested, had gathered around Don Bosco. Spaventa, feeling that their sympathies were with the priest, invited him into his room and asked him to sit down.

"I know that you do a great deal of good," he said, changing his tone; "what can I do for you?"

"I should be grateful if you would explain the reason for the inquisitorial visits I have received and the persecution to which I have been subjected."

"Well, you know—your political opinions—I am not at liberty to say more, but I can give you a hint. If you would speak plainly and reveal your secrets you would be all right."

"What secrets?"

"The Jesuitical secrets, which the police were searching for."

"I know nothing about them. If you will speak to me openly, I will reply in the same manner."

"Oh, I can't meddle in the matter. Ask the Minister."

"Well, if you can't help me in any other way,

will you obtain for me an audience with the Minister?"

"I will see what I can do. In the meantime, don't speak to anyone on this subject."

He left the room. In half an hour he was back. The Minister was engaged, he said, and could not see Don Bosco. So he went home, still fasting. It was 8 o'clock.

Next morning came a letter saying that Farini would see Don Bosco at 11 o'clock the following day. It happened to be the Feast of Our Lady of Mount Carmel. The boys were told to pray hard for "a special intention," for which they offered their Mass and Communion.

Farini was quite gracious. He spoke of the good Don Bosco was doing for the poor boys of Turin and asked what he could do for him.

"Tell me," said Don Bosco, "the reason for all the visits I have been receiving."

"Certainly. As long as you confined yourself to looking after your poor children, the Government thoroughly appreciated your work, but since you have taken to meddling with politics we are obliged to watch you."

"All my life long," said Don Bosco, "I have made it my aim to keep out of politics. Will you kindly tell me which of my actions you consider suspicious?"

"The articles that you write in the paper, the

Armonia, the reactionary assemblies held in your house and your correspondence with the enemies of the nation."

"May I answer you as frankly as you have spoken to me?" asked Don Bosco. "I know of no law which forbids me to write articles for the *Armonia* or any other paper; but, as a matter of fact, I can assure Your Excellency that I have written no articles for any paper."

"However much you deny it," said the Minister, "I can prove that many of the articles in that paper are yours."

"I do not fear your proofs, Excellency, for they have no foundation," replied Don Bosco.

"Do you mean to say that I am a liar?"

"No. You only believe what you have been told. The blame lies with the people who willfully misrepresent the facts."

"But Father, are you aware that in censuring my subordinates, you are censuring the Government itself?"

"If Your Excellency can prove me mistaken I will withdraw my statement."

"A good citizen does not blame public authority."

"I have no intention of blaming anyone. I am merely defending myself against false accusations—pure inventions of malicious men to deceive the authorities and to cause them to act unjustly and arbitrarily."

Farini was amazed at Don Bosco's boldness.

"You do not realize," he said, "that you are speaking to a Minister, who could send you to prison."

"Your Excellency loves honor and justice too well to imprison an innocent citizen whose only aim is to do good to his neighbor."

"Can you affirm on your conscience that no reactionary meetings have been held in your house, and that you do not keep up a political correspondence with the Jesuits, Archbishop Franzoni and the court of Rome?"

Don Bosco assured him that such reports were false. He did not even know the Jesuits' address, and his relations with the Archbishop and the Pope were those which every priest was bound to have with his ecclesiastical superiors.

"We have proofs to the contrary," said Farini.

"I have the right to ask for them to be produced," said Don Bosco. "I demand justice."

At this moment, the door opened and Count Cavour came in. Don Bosco was relieved, as the Count, though his opinions were those of Farini, had often befriended him. He poured out the whole story of the persecution and emphasized the harm it was doing to the Oratory. Cavour assured him that no harm was intended, but renewed the accusations of Farini. Don Bosco's principles and the spirit of his Institute were contrary to the politics of the Government.

"I have lived for 20 years in Turin," said Don Bosco, "and I defy anyone to produce a line or word or act of mine against the Government."

"Come, come," said Farini, "you will never convince me that you share our ideas."

"Would you carry tyranny so far as to punish a man for his private opinions?" exclaimed Don Bosco. "I can only reaffirm that I have never said or done anything that could lead anyone to consider me the enemy of the State. Furthermore, I have been doing my best to cooperate with the Government by bringing up destitute boys to earn an honest livelihood instead of becoming a danger to society and to the State. These are my politics—I have no others."

The Ministers seemed impressed. They declared that in the future, Don Bosco would be left in peace to look after his children. They even asked for his prayers.

But his trials were not over yet. After a little period of peace, his enemies began again. On this occasion, his chief opponents were Gatti, an official in the Ministry of Public Instruction, and Selmi, Chief Educational Officer for Turin. Their aim was to make him close his schools, and to obtain this result they accused him of employing professors who had no legal diploma.

He was ordered by Selmi to send in a list of his teachers with their certificates. Don Bosco sent in their names and explained that they were taking means to obtain certificates by attending classes at the University of Turin. As the schools were for the benefit of poor boys, he said, he had been given authority by the Minister of Public Instruction to go on as he was doing for the present. Selmi refused to admit this plea, declaring that Don Bosco must at once produce certified teachers or close his schools. He appealed against this decision, but in vain.

Finally it was suggested that he could at once present his schoolmasters for an examination as to their fitness to teach. But when Gatti found, to his disgust, that this proposal was welcomed, he resolved to find means to prevent their being admitted. Sure now that Gatti was determined to close the schools, Don Bosco proceeded to apply to Selmi, who had power to certify teachers for one year provisionally.

Selmi received him with studied rudeness. After a long rigmarole against priests, the Pope, the Jesuits, Don Bosco himself and his schools, received by Don Bosco with smiling patience, he burst out, "I am angry, as you see, and yet you smile!"

"What you say does not concern me."

"Not concern you? Are you not Don Bosco,

the famous Jesuit and teacher of Jesuits?"

"No," said Don Bosco, "I am not, and I beg of you to give me a patient hearing."

"What are these schools, for which you ask favors?"

Don Bosco explained that they consisted of poor children from all over Italy who were being educated or being taught a trade, and that he had, including the day students, over 1,000.

"Who pays for keeping these boys?"

"I receive no payment but what is given me in charity, and I have to work hard to obtain means to find it."

Selmi calmed down. "I have been misinformed," he said. "But why are you so hostile to the Government?"

Don Bosco declared that he had never shown a trace of hostility to the Government, that some of his best friends had been ministers, and that in earlier days the Government had approved and helped his work.

The conversation continued, Selmi becoming more and more reasonable. Presently he asked Don Bosco to state what were his difficulties about submitting to the educational authorities.

"I only asked for the present teachers to be allowed to continue with their classes until they can obtain their certificates," was the answer, and Selmi at once gave the required permission.

On receipt of their names, he said, he would send a formal certificate of approval. Don Bosco invited him to come and see the Oratory, and the two parted with the utmost cordiality.

Selmi kept his word, but Don Bosco had still Gatti to deal with, and Gatti declared that the teachers in question could neither be allowed to continue teaching nor be admitted to the public examinations, as they had not attended the classes at the university regularly. Don Bosco pointed out that this was not true.

"I cannot understand you," he said; "you first say that my teachers must undergo the public examination before they can be certified, and you now refuse them permission to go up for examination."

"That was said before the matter had been investigated," said Gatti. "It has now been decided otherwise."

This looked more than a little like ill will.

"What am I to do?" asked Don Bosco.

"You must engage certified professors at once."

"But I cannot find them, and if I could, I could not pay them."

"Then it only remains to close your schools."

"For this year, at least, I can keep them open; next year I will see what can be done."

"By whose authority can you keep the schools open?"

"By that of the chief Education Officer."

"Signor Selmi has no right to meddle in this affair."

"But he has authorized my present teachers for this year."

Don Bosco showed him the paper—Gatti raged.

"He is an ignoramus and must be kept in his place," he said.

"All I know," said Don Bosco, "is that for the scholastic affairs of the Province of Turin, he is the authority to whom we must apply."

He took his leave of Gatti and went to Selmi to report what had happened. Selmi was exceedingly angry. He told Don Bosco to go home in peace as it would be all right.

Gatti and Selmi now began an abusive correspondence, while Don Bosco's teachers went on teaching. When the time came for their examination, a written refusal to admit them was sent to Don Bosco, against which he immediately appealed. The result of this was a fresh visit of inspection which lasted two days.

Everything went off well, and the Inspector declared himself completely satisfied with all that he had seen and heard. It was therefore a painful surprise when, a few days later, Don Bosco was informed that the extremely unfavorable report of the Inspector had confirmed the Ministry in

their belief that the Oratory was a nest of sedition. Don Bosco, still undaunted, now paid a
visit to Amati, the Minister of Public Instruction, to whom the report had been sent.

"What can I do for you, Father?" he asked.

"I am being continually plagued by inquisitorial visits," said Don Bosco, "and I want to
know why. I have always been loyal to the King."

"Who are you?"

"I am Don Bosco, Director of the Oratory of
St. Francis de Sales for the education and training of poor boys."

"I hear that your establishment has degener-
ated into a school of reactionaries, disobedient
to lawful authority. That is why I ordered a visit
of inspection."

"It has been going on for three years," said
Don Bosco, "and it is a persecution rather than
an inspection. The boys were even urged to dis-
close their inmost thoughts."

"That was not the kind of inspection I
ordered," said the Minister. He rang his bell and
asked that Gatti and the Inspector be summoned.
They came in and, as it was dark, sat down
without noticing that Don Bosco was there.

"What was the result of your visit to the
Oratory?" asked the Minister, turning to the
Inspector.

"As you will see from the report," replied the

Inspector, "a very evil influence is prevalent there."

"What have you to report about the teaching?"

"Just think, Excellency, there was not a portrait of the King in the house!"

"What about the teaching?" repeated Amati with some impatience.

"He has obtained a decree of approbation which allows the school to remain open for this year," said Gatti, "but we have every reason to hope that it will turn out to be illegal."

"Supposing we hear what Don Bosco has to say about it," said the Minister, turning to where Don Bosco stood in the shadows.

The two accomplices looked decidedly caught as he stepped forward. The Inspector who, after praising the Institute to the skies to Don Bosco's face had written such an untrue report behind his back, hardly knew where to look, while Gatti, claiming he had an appointment, beat a hasty retreat.

"Speak out, Don Bosco," said Amati, and Don Bosco gave a full account of all he had had to suffer, ending with the assurance that there were no less than three portraits of the King in the house.

"It amounts to a concealment of truth and a distortion of facts," he concluded, "which is calculated to entirely deceive the Government."

It was easy enough to see where honesty lay. The Minister dismissed the Inspector curtly and turned to Don Bosco.

"I have had a warning," he said, "to be careful in the choice of my subordinates, but I can't understand how all these mischievous reports got about. Is there any secret reason for them? If you will tell me, I might be able to help you."

Don Bosco assured him that they were malicious inventions, disseminated by the enemies of religion. He devoted himself entirely to the welfare of his boys and his work in the prisons and the hospitals, and he thought he had been badly treated by those from whom he might have expected help and consideration.

After a long and friendly conversation, Amati ended by assuring him that as long as he was Minister of Public Instruction, Don Bosco could count on his help and protection.

So, through much tribulation, peace came in the end. The Government at last realized that Don Bosco and men like him could combine the duties of a good Catholic with those of a loyal citizen. Moreover, Don Bosco had learned exactly what the new laws required, and he was the first to send in his clerics and priests to the public examinations, in which his students scored a brilliant success.

During these troublous times, he must have

often remembered the words of his mother: "When you begin to say Mass, you begin to carry the Cross." He had carried it all his life, but, no matter how heavy he had found it, he never dragged it. He bore it bravely, shoulder-high, and as his life went on it grew heavier and pressed in different ways. Physical infirmities weighed upon a body that had been wholly used in the service of God. His sight began to fail, until in time all writing was forbidden him. He grew lame, persistent arthritis and affliction of the spine bent his strong frame, but there was no question of giving in. While there was an ounce of life in him that could still be used in the service of souls, he would use it. The long hours in the confessional went on as before, at what cost to himself he alone knew.

His family was growing up around him strong and helpful, and there was his right hand, his beloved Don Rua, always beside him to share a burden that was growing too heavy for his failing strength alone. He could look back on the years—on the work God had given him to do—with a song of praise and thanksgiving. Our Lady, Help of Christians had, as always, been faithful to the trust he had placed in her.

"You have been burning the candle at both ends all your life," said a famous doctor who had been called in toward the end of his life to see what could be done. "Your body is like a worn-out coat that is absolutely threadbare. There is nothing for it but rest—complete rest."

"That is the one remedy that is impossible," was the answer. "I have too much work to do." He would go on to the very end. While there were souls to be saved, there would be no rest for him. "We will rest in Heaven," he had said once long ago to an anxious friend. When he could no longer stand, *then* he would no longer go.

Chapter 9

THE GREAT ACHIEVEMENT

IN HIS rescue work among the poor boys of Turin, the equally urgent needs of the girls must have often struck Don Bosco. It struck others too, and both priests and laymen never ceased to urge him to found a Congregation of women on the same lines as the Salesian Order to do for destitute girls what it was doing for boys.

The beginnings of this enterprise came about, one might almost say, by accident. On one of his frequent journeys, it happened that Don Bosco met in the train Don Pestarino, the parish priest of Mornese, who in his little country district had inaugurated an association of young girls who wanted to devote themselves to the service of others without becoming nuns. The two men entered into conversation and began to talk about what was nearest to their hearts— their apostolic work. Don Bosco, who was immensely interested in the enterprise of Don Pestarino, put himself in touch with the little group of girls at Mornese and never ceased to follow its development. Maria Mazzarello, a simple country girl who had been the first to join, fell ill a little later with a bad attack of typhoid fever, which left her much less robust than she had been before.

"I can no longer work in the vineyards," she said one day to a friend; "I am thinking of serving an apprenticeship to the village tailor. I should then be able to teach the children to work as well as to save their souls." Her friend determined to join her. They agreed between themselves that they would set in every stitch for the love of God, and went to the church to ask a blessing on their enterprise. At the end of the year, the two girls knew enough to begin to teach. They were joined by others, and the country people began to send them their children. To save time and work, they had their meals together, prayed together and took up their abode in a house close to the church. They were visited periodically by Don Bosco, who in 1871, having asked counsel of the Pope as to the founding of the suggested Order for women and having received unreserved approval, definitely made up his mind.

On the 29th of January, 1872, Feast of St. Francis de Sales, the Community, 27 in number, met in chapter and elected their superior,

Maria Mazzarello, who was chosen by a majority of 15. It only remained to give a name and a habit to the little company, but Don Bosco had named them already in his heart—they were to be the Daughters of Our Lady, Help of Christians. Nine years later Don Bosco removed them—now 69 in number, to Nizza Monferrato, where they began to do for girls all the different things that the Salesians were doing for boys, plus a few others such as running nurseries, hospitals, retreat houses for ladies, summer camps and homes for working girls, besides taking charge of the cooking, laundry work and mending in most of the Salesian houses. In 1877, they followed the Salesians to America, and in 1890 went to help them in their mission work in Patagonia and Brazil. Later, the motherhouse was moved to Turin, where it was established close to that of the Salesians.

But that is looking too far into the future: it is necessary to go back to the founding of the Salesian missions, a work so dear to Don Bosco.

By 1875, he was 60 and had gone through an almost superhuman amount of work. It might have seemed to most men that he had earned his rest. Two large and ever-increasing Congregations of men and women had spread themselves over half of Europe and were laboring at all the causes that he had at heart. No—not quite all. Twenty years earlier, one of his first disciples, coming into his room, had found him lost in contemplation before a picture he had just hung on the wall. "Who is it?" he asked. "A great missionary," was the reply, "Gabriel Perboyre, martyred a few years ago in China." The two stood before it in silence—a silence that was broken by a whisper from Don Bosco, apparently talking to himself: "Oh, if I had only a dozen priests after my own heart, we would start at once together."

It may have been this very disciple, John Cagliero, who lay dying in 1854, the year of the cholera epidemic in Turin. He had been one of the most zealous workers among the stricken, and the terrible attack of typhoid from which he was suffering was the direct outcome of his labors. Don Bosco, warned by the doctors that they could do nothing more for him, went to his bedside.

"Come, John," he said, "do you want to live or go to Heaven?"

"To go to Heaven," was the prompt answer.

"Well, you won't—not this time. Our Blessed Lady is going to cure you. You will recover, you will be a priest, and one day, breviary in hand, you will go—far—far away."

The eyes of Don Bosco seemed to be looking wonderingly into the future as if he saw many things—and strange. It was not till several years later that he confessed what he had seen. Over the pillow where that dear son was lying, there fluttered a dove with a branch of olive in its beak, which it drew gently once or twice across the boy's lips. In the distance hovered a group of Indians, from which two gigantic warriors, one black-skinned, the other red, detached themselves to bend over the dying boy, as if listening eagerly for his failing breath. The dove foreshadowed the pouring out of the Gifts of the Holy Spirit upon John Cagliero at his consecration as bishop; the warriors were to be the sheep of his flock.

Sixteen years later, another of these wonderfully prophetic dreams of Don Bosco confirmed the earlier vision. It seemed to him that he was in a wild savage land, bounded in the distance by a range of high mountains. This country—which he saw with extraordinary vividness—was peopled with half-naked savages of ferocious aspect. Some were racing, some hunting, others fighting with each other or with European soldiers, others carried bleeding fragments of flesh impaled on their spears. Presently, there appeared in the distance a group of men whom Don Bosco recognized as missionaries. They approached the natives in a friendly manner but were immediately attacked, killed and hacked into pieces to an accompaniment of wild howls and yells.

Don Bosco was wondering whether it would ever be possible to convert such a race as this when he was aware of another band approaching. Among these, he was able to discern a few familiar faces, for they were Salesians. He would have beckoned to them to warn them to go back, fearing that they would meet the same fate as their predecessors, when, to his great astonishment, the wild men began to show signs of friendliness. They laid down their arms and welcomed the new arrivals as if they were pleased to see them.

In a little while the savages were gathered around the missionaries listening to their teachings and learning their prayers like little children. Later again they were saying the Rosary all together and singing the hymns of the Church with such vigor and enthusiasm that Don Bosco awoke, to find himself in his own bed. "I knew then," he said, "that one day my sons would be at work in the mission fields, but I often asked myself the question: *Where*, and who are these wild men to whom they will preach the Faith?"

The answer came in 1874, when the Archbishop of Buenos Aires offered him the evangelization of the wilder regions of South America, Patagonia and Tierra del Fuego. He immediately realized that these were the people of his dream.

In December, 1875, John Cagliero—the little lad whom Don Bosco had picked up on one of his visits to Castelnuovo, his own country, and had brought back to the Oratory to be educated under his own eyes—was consecrated Bishop in the great Church of Mary, Help of Christians. As the new Bishop came down from the sanctuary, the first person he met was his old mother, aged 88, just such another as Margaret Bosco. The little old lady disappeared almost entirely in the arms of her tall son, whose newly acquired episcopal dignity did not forbid a thoroughly filial embrace.

Cagliero then turned to Don Bosco who stood awaiting him, bareheaded. His consecrated hands were hidden under his vestments, for he had not allowed even his mother to kiss the episcopal ring. Don Bosco made an effort to possess himself of it, but Bishop Cagliero gave him no time. Father and son were in each other's arms, both weeping tears of joy. It was he who was chosen to lead the first little band of Salesian missionaries—ten in number, a mere handful of men to evangelize a country as large as France twice over, plus Belgium. But they were all Don Bosco could spare at the moment, and they were full of zeal.

Don Bosco went with them to Genoa and stayed with them till the ship set sail.

"Think of nothing but souls," he said to them as he sent them off, "and make no account of all the rest. Be very kind to children, the sick, the old and the wretched. Submit loyally in all things to your ecclesiastical and civil superiors. Trust in the power of the Holy Eucharist and our Blessed Lady. Do what you can, and leave the rest to God."

Year by year, slowly and steadily, the number of missionaries increased. It was not easy work. All the obstacles of a savage and pagan race had to be gradually overcome. The native peoples were fierce and cruel by nature, though not without fine qualities. In 20 years, the whole of Patagonia had been won for Christ, and the great Vicariate of Magellan, Pampa and Patagonia established.

When Don Bosco was in France in 1883, he spoke to the Geographical Society of Lyons on the subject of Patagonia and the work that was being done there. His descriptions were so vivid and his information so exact that they asked him how he could have possibly obtained it without being on the spot. He showed some confusion and hesitated for a moment. "All I have told you is true," he said evasively. He had simply related what he had seen in one of his dreams.

The missionaries now began to look further afield, toward the Asiatic tribes of the Equator, far beyond the bounds of civilization. In 1895, under a Salesian bishop, another great vicariate took shape, that of Mendez and Gualaquiza.

A year earlier, the sons of Don Bosco had penetrated into the heart of Brazil among the widely dispersed Indian tribes who were still pagan. After 20 years of arduous labor, they had succeeded in forming the Prelature of Araguaza with another Salesian bishop at its head. The Apostolic Prefecture of Rio Negro followed. Within ten years they were in Paraguay, where such magnificent work had been done by the Jesuits—and destroyed—working among the marches of Gran Chaco.

It looked as if the evangelization of the Indians was to be the great work of the Salesian Order, an arduous task, but one for which there was urgent need. Other races had conquered their lands, but few had troubled about their souls—outside of that gallant band of Jesuit missionaries who had suffered martyrdom after unspeakable tortures in the early days of French colonization in Canada. Driven farther and farther into the wild at the approach of the conquerors, robbed of their heritage and learning from the white man degradation rather than civilization, they had sore need of the consolations of the Faith.

Yet the work of the Salesians was not to stop

there. In 1911, the Salesians of Belgium were asked by their government to establish themselves in the province of Katanga in the Belgian Congo. So fruitful was their work that 14 years later their mission field was raised to the rank of an Apostolic Prefecture—that of High Luapula.

There remained China—the first dream of Don Bosco. In 1920, the Apostolic Vicariate of Shiu Chow was founded in central China and offered to the zeal of the Salesians. In the same year, they took over the Apostolic Prefecture of Assam, and eight years later the diocese and archdiocese of Krishnagar and Malacca. The original ten who had set out for Patagonia had grown in the course of years to over 2,000, counting the Daughters of Our Lady, Help of Christians who had joined them two years after their arrival. Four years after the raising of this first mission field to the rank of an Apostolic Vicariate, Don Bosco died, but he had foreseen it all in a dream. "This is the harvest reserved for the Salesians," he had been told, as he saw before him the great districts of South America that were still pagan. Three years later, in 1886, it was the beautiful Shepherdess of his earlier dreams who showed him vast lands in Africa and China where his sons were to penetrate, carrying with them the gift of Faith. "Too great a field, too great," he had said, thinking of the poverty of his little army. "No," she had said, "be at rest; not your sons only, but the sons of your sons and their sons after them will carry on the work." Dreams were not his only consolation. Great was his joy when he was told that John Cagliero, that son of his predilection, was returning home after 13 years spent in the mission field, and not alone. Hardly was that joyous meeting over when the door opened and a little Indian girl from Tierra del Fuego walked in. Kneeling at Don Bosco's feet, she looked at him affectionately. "Father," she said, "I thank you with all my heart for sending your missionaries for my salvation and that of my people." It was one of the happiest moments of Don Bosco's life.

Weary and ailing as he was, he managed in 1886 to take a journey to Spain to visit the Spanish houses of the Order and his many friends. He was received with the greatest enthusiasm— a welcome worthy of a king. There were the same streams of visitors, the same crowds fighting to get near him as in France. People of all classes sat by the roadside where he was to pass, waiting for a blessing or a touch of his hand or garments. Toward the end of his visit, they made him stand in the balcony and bless the crowds that streamed past in the street below. And the same wonders repeated themselves. A young girl of 15 whose right leg and hand were completely twisted was brought to him. Don Bosco blessed her. "Just walk," he said, and she did it, opening and shutting the hand that she had never been able to move. A mother with her three children asked him to bless them and to pray that they might always be faithful to Christ. He gave them a long look, and raised his eyes to Heaven. "These two big boys will be religious," he said, "and the baby will be for me." In 1900, the "baby," now grown up, became a Salesian. His two brothers had been in religion for some time.

In 1887, Don Bosco was in Rome for the consecration of the Church of the Sacred Heart, where he said Mass at Our Lady's altar. The Mass was long, for the holy old man was weeping tears of joy all through it. His secretary asked him why, since the completed church was the glorious end of a great effort. "Because," said the Saint, "I had all the time before my eyes that first dream that was the key to my whole life—those boys like wild beasts—that heavenly Shepherdess who transformed them into lambs, her injunctions to me: 'By kindness and gentleness you must win them.' And one word above all was ringing in my ears, her answer when I begged her to give me the key to what I saw: 'One day, in God's good time, you will understand.' That was 60 years ago, and I understand today."

There in the Eternal City, as he offered the Holy Sacrifice in the church of his prayers and his labors, the whole field of his life's work lay open before him and he understood.

He understood, too, that his work was nearly over. He walked no longer but rather dragged himself along, leaning on the arm of one of his sons. The heart and will alone remained full of life, and they belonged, as they always had, to his children.

"Do you know what I ask for you?" he wrote to them from Rome. "That you may believe and act as I have taught you to do. Some day you will learn what a privilege it is to be in a Salesian house. I tell you that if a boy or young man comes into one of our houses, Our Lady, Help of Christians takes him under her very special protection. Let me have the joy of knowing you are faithful; the time is near when I shall leave you and pass into my eternity."

In the November of 1887, after a retreat at Valsalice in Turin at which he had insisted on being present, in spite of his growing weakness, he said a few words of farewell which they only understood later. "Now that it has been decided that the scholasticate for the philosophy of our young religious is to be here, we shall see you more often, shall we not?" they asked. "Yes, I shall come here, I shall remain here as guardian," and he looked at the stairway which led from the terrace to the great courtyard. Four months later, they were digging his grave on that very spot. As he said himself, he might go now. Others had been formed to take his place. The Salesian Congregation counted 38 houses in Europe and 26 in America. On the morrow, Don Bosco was to give the habit to four new disciples, two Poles, one Frenchman and an Englishman.

One of the last visits he paid was to the nuns of the Sacred Heart, driven out of the country by the anti-religious Government in 1848. In 1884, they had returned as Don Bosco had prophesied they would and had opened a new house at Valsalice, close to the Salesians. As their arrival coincided with the consecration of the great Church of Our Lady, Help of Christians, they had dedicated their convent to the Blessed Virgin under that title and had placed it under her powerful protection.

A month later, Don Bosco could no longer say Mass, even in his private oratory, but that December brought him a last great joy. A new band of missionaries—the 12th since 1875—was about to depart for Quito, and Don Bosco, leaning on his secretary, came to the church to hear the sermon and to bless the new apostles. Scarcely had they gone when Bishop Cagliero arrived from America, a journey undertaken with the greatest difficulty. During a visitation of his diocese, riding in the Cordilleras, he had had a terrible fall, breaking two ribs and bringing him to death's door. Through the dangerous illness that followed, he had never given up hope, for it seemed to him that he heard continually a voice that said: "Go to Turin to be with Don Bosco at his death."

On the evening of that day, Don Bosco was for the last time with his sons in the community refectory. One by one all the little joys of family life were to be denied him.

For 40 years, he had given every morning to the blessing, comforting, helping and advising of all who came to see him—and they were many. To within a month of his death, he kept up this practice, no matter how much it cost him in pain and weariness. A friend who came to see him during these days chronicles his astonishment at finding in an old man who was almost dying so vivid and sympathetic an interest in every trouble or difficulty of his visitors. "The keen sword of the spirit has worn out the sheath, but what strength of soul there is still in that feeble body!" Although he had been obliged some years before to give up the long morning Confessions, he still continued to hear them on two evenings a week, but soon this too proved too much for his failing strength. On the 17th of December, a little more than a month before his death, they told him that some 30 of his boys, old enough to be thinking seriously of their future life, were begging to see him. They had been told that he was too ill, but they still persisted. When his secretary went to Don Bosco with their message, he hesitated, but only for a moment. "Let them in," he said, "it will be for the last time." And when the secretary, very unwilling, urged the pain and weariness under which the old man was almost sinking, he repeated, "It will be the last time, tell them to come." He had spoken the truth; those were the last Confessions that he heard.

During those last days of suffering, the thought of the missions was continually in his mind.

"Tell everyone," he said to Bishop Cagliero, "that to come to the help of the missions is an infallible way to obtain from Our Lady the graces that we desire. Remind so-and-so not to forget the missions, and I will not forget him and his."

"Don't be afraid," he said again in one of those flashes of insight that were peculiar to him; "you will go to Africa, from end to end—to Asia, to Mongolia and farther still. Wherever you go, preach devotion to Our Lady. If you only knew how many souls she will bring to God through the means of the Salesian Congregation!"

And only four days before his death, in one last burst of energy he whispered to Bishop Cagliero, kneeling beside his bed, "Save many souls on the missions." "I shall always remember," he said on another occasion, "what our Cooperators have done for the missions."

The Union of Salesian Cooperators, founded in 1876, was another instance of Don Bosco's indefatigable zeal. Everyone who was ready to help in any way in the salvation of souls, men or women, no matter of what age or rank in life, might belong to it. It had its first beginning in the devoted little group of men and women who united to help Don Bosco in his early work at Valdocco. His keen insight realized that there were cases and situations where the help of a lay man or woman might be more efficacious than that of a priest, where one might prepare the way for the other.

The lay apostolate, for which there is so much need in these days, was in Don Bosco's mind when he drew up the rules for his Cooperators, who were to be so powerful an aid to him in all his enterprises. Some could help by prayer, others by alms, others by their generously given gifts and talents, small or great as they happened to be. Others, and these not the least precious, could help by pain, weariness and suffering generously borne and offered in union with the suffering of Our Lord upon the Cross. In all works, merits and enterprises of the Order, the Cooperators were to have their share; they belonged to the Salesian family.

The whole of Italy, one might almost say the whole world, was praying that Don Bosco might be left a little longer in the world. The house was besieged by crowds eager for news of the invalid. A noble lady of Turin, calling to hear the latest bulletin, was presented by the porter with the daily paper, which announced an amelioration. "Oh, tell him to get well," she cried, bursting into tears, "and give him this," and she thrust a well-filled purse into the porter's hand.

As for the invalid himself, he was peacefully waiting for the end.

"Tell me just how it is going," he said to the doctors, "you know I am not afraid. I am quite ready and quite content."

"Do they know in the house how ill I am?" he asked his secretary.

"Yes, Don Bosco, not only in this house, but in all our houses, and they are all praying."

"For my recovery? It will not be. I am passing to my eternity."

"I am longing to go to Heaven," he said on another occasion, "for there I shall be able to do something for my children. Here I can no longer work for them."

The doctors said frankly that there was no hope. "His life has been sapped by labors above his strength," they said. "There is no real illness, the lamp is going out for want of oil."

No one knew it better than Don Bosco himself. He begged all who came to see him to help him to "save his poor soul."

"What, my dear Don Bosco," said Cardinal Alimonda, "you surely do not fear death, you who have so often prepared others and bidden them hold themselves ready?"

"I have said it to others, Your Eminence, and now I need that others should say it to me."

On the 3rd of December, he received the last Sacraments. "Pray for me, all of you," he said to the priests gathered around his bed, "that I may receive my Lord as He should be received; my mind is not clear. *In manus tuas, Domine, commendo spiritum meum* ('Into Your hands, O Lord, I commend my spirit')." Bishop Cagliero, bearing the Sacred Host, approached him, hardly able to control his tears. . . .

In spite of weakness and suffering, Don Bosco retained his presence of mind and cheery spirit. After a spell of weakness that reduced him to a state of temporary unconsciousness, sometimes of long duration, he would begin to speak of the affairs of the Congregation with a lucidity and intelligence that astonished those about him, no less than did his unvarying smile. One day he would make a witty verse on the incapacity of his legs. "Put it all on the bill," he said to one of his sons who had the privilege of lifting him from one couch to another. "I will settle it all with a lump sum—at the end." And another day, even when he was fighting for breath: "Don't any of you know of a bellows factory?"

"But why?" they asked, rather at a loss.

"Why? To place an order for two new lungs; mine are not worth a cent between them."

"I am afraid we are causing you much suffering," they said once, when they had moved him from one bed to another. "Oh, that goes without saying," he said with a smile, and he kept that smile till the end. One thing only brought a cloud over his serenity—his fatherly heart ached at the thought of the separation from those he loved. "The only sacrifice I shall have to make," he said, "is leaving you."

"Take from the pocket of my soutane my purse and my pocket-book," he said one day toward the end, "and give them to Don Rua. I want to die as poor as I have lived." But the thought of their poverty hurt him. "My children are still asking for bread," he said, "and I can no longer beg for them. Those who want to help them must not wait for me to come."

One night when Don Rua and Bishop Cagliero were kneeling at his bedside, he gave them his last message for all his sons. "Live together as brothers, love each other and bear with each other. The protection of Our Lady, Help of Christians, will always be with you." On New Year's Eve, when Don Rua asked him what memento he would like to give to his children, he said, "Devotion to our Blessed Lady and frequent Communion"—the two great means of holiness of life that he had spent his days inculcating. Even in moments of delirium, his soul spoke. "Pray!" he cried one night, just before his death, "pray, but with faith—with living faith! Courage, courage! Onward, ever onward!"

His last words, spoken with calm lucidity and from his heart, were for his dear boys. "Tell them that I shall wait for them all in Paradise," he said. "Frequent Communion and devotion to Our Lady will be their safeguard." "When I can speak no more," he said to his secretary, "and someone comes to ask my blessing, lift up my hand and make with it the Sign of the Cross. I will make the intention."

They gathered all around his bed in mute agony, waiting for the end. The Crucifix was on his breast and the white stole across his feet. One by one they passed, kissing the thin hand that lay outside the coverlet.

"Don Bosco," said Bishop Cagliero, "we your sons are here. We ask your pardon for all the pain we may at any time have caused you. As a sign of forgiveness, give us once more your blessing. I will guide your hand." They bent to receive it with breaking hearts as Bishop Cagliero lifted the paralyzed hand and made the Sign of the Cross. The agony began: "Jesus, Mary, Joseph, I give you my heart and my soul," prayed Bishop Cagliero. At half-past four, Don Bosco gave a gentle sigh and ceased to breathe. It was January 31, 1888. As he was poor in life, he was poor in death. The Oratory, with its 800 mouths to feed, was obliged on the very day he died to beg the baker to give the daily bread on credit.

Chapter 10

THE SPREAD OF THE WORK

THEY BURIED him in the center of the great stairway leading from the courtyard to the terrace, in the very place he had pointed out four months before. They laid the coffin in the grave and Bishop Cagliero, his missionary bishop, spoke. "Even as the first Christians gained at the tombs of the martyrs strength for the last fight, so will people come to this grave to seek light and strength, energy, rectitude of life and devotion to all great causes."

Well might his sons be proud of such a Father. He was dead, but his work lived on. In Heaven, he heard the prayers of the multitude that continued to appeal to him for help in all kinds of trouble and distress, and the marvelous answers went on as they had done when he was alive. He was already a saint by general acclaim when two years later the preliminaries of his cause began in Turin. He had been dead only 21 years when Pope Pius X declared him Venerable, and in 1929 he was beatified by Pope Pius XI.

"In all the years that I have been attached to the Vatican," said Archbishop Salotti, Secretary of the Sacred Congregation for the Propagation of the Faith, "never have I witnessed such scenes as I have witnessed today. What will the crowds be like when Don Bosco is canonized?" That question was answered on Easter Sunday, 1934. Eighty thousand people from all over the world were present within the great church of St. Peter's, and innumerable thousands packed the great Square outside, through which Pope Pius XI, with characteristic thoughtfulness, had himself borne, that those who could not get in to the basilica might not be disappointed. Never was the banner of Saint hailed with such deafening applause as was the picture of St. John Bosco, as it moved with slow solemnity through the middle of the immense crowded nave. The great lights on pillar and dado—everywhere—made one think of the Saint in his actual dwelling place in Heaven's glowing light and glory. "God gave him largeness of heart as the sand on the seashore," the Pope wrote of the Saint.

"Don Bosco came among us," he said in his audience to the Salesians, "to render to the Divine Redeemer all that is owing to Him. From Him all that remains of good in the world—even a half-pagan world—takes its rise. All that remains of good civilization comes from the Cross, from the Heart and Blood of the Redeemer, and on this account it is still a Christian civilization. The Redeemer Himself has told us what should be the fruit of all His work of Redemption— the continuation of that Redemption itself. Don Bosco says to you today: 'Live the Christian life as we have lived it and taught it.' Don Bosco's love of the Redeemer became love of the souls which He has redeemed at the price of His Precious Blood, and he points out to you the great and powerful help on which you must count to carry out that love of Christ which translates itself into love for souls. Mary, Help of Christians, is your inheritance. One of the most precious fruits of the Redemption is the Motherhood of Mary. It is the Divine Redeemer who has given us Mary as our universal Mother. Here is a help which has no limitations to its power— Mary, our Mother, who desires nothing more than to lend her aid to the good works which we desire to do for the glory of God and the good of souls."

The Church had bestowed the greatest honor it could confer on the little peasant boy of Becchi. It remained for the State to do the same, both in Rome and Turin. The Crown Prince of Italy was present at the Canonization as the representative of the King. In the bitterest days of Italy's anti-clericalism, Don Bosco had stood like a link between Catholicism and the State. It was therefore fitting that there should be a great civic gathering in the capitol of Rome, at which the highest dignitaries of Church and State were present and at which Count de Vecchi, concluding an eloquent speech, made a remark very apposite of our own day. He referred to the part Don Bosco had played as mediator between Church and State and concluded by saying that Don Bosco was "one more proof that the greatest diplomat is the man of prayer—a lesson which the world has still to learn today."

St. John Bosco had once dreamt that he found himself in a strange machine flying over Latin America, accompanied by a guide who made sure he took note of the immense natural resources hitherto untapped by man. Here was but a foretaste of what lay in store for these rich countries and for Don Bosco's spiritual sons, the Salesians.

The mysterious guide pointed to a line on the map that started at Valparaiso and cut across the heart of Africa, joining Calcutta, Hong Kong and Peking. "Along this line," his guide told him, "will rise ten very important Salesian centers." But Don Bosco could contain himself no longer. More! He wanted to see and know more. Almost with a pinch of impatience he blurted out: "And Boston! When do we go to Boston?"

Not heeding his question, his guide said, "Come, I want you to see the triumphs that await the Society of St. Francis de Sales. Climb this rock and you will see for yourself." From the top of the huge boulder, Don Bosco saw a boundless plain. As far as the eye could reach, he saw Salesians leading groups of boys and girls followed by an immense crowd. He saw some he knew, but many more whom he did not know. Still he persisted: "But aren't they waiting for us in Boston?" His guide only replied, "You will understand everything in due time."

Today that dream is a reality. In 1,500 centers throughout the world, 17,000 Salesians are carrying out the task of saving the souls of boys that Don Bosco started in 1841 in Turin, Italy. And although Don Bosco never crossed the ocean himself, he was to fulfill his lifelong desire by sending his sons as missionaries to many far-off countries.

During his lifetime, Don Bosco had the joy of seeing eight missionary bands go forth to bring the glad tidings to poor pagan lands where the name of Christ was unknown. As Don Bosco's right-hand man, and eventually his successor, Father Rua—now Blessed Michael Rua—seems to have inherited the same propelling urge to bring the light of the Gospel to those who groped in darkness. He cast such a lasting and indispensable influence over the development of the Society that in 20 years, its foundations were multiplied fivefold.

It was during Don Rua's tenure of office that the Salesians arrived in the United States. This was in 1897. On the west coast, they came from Venezuela up through Mexico to San Francisco, where they established the Province of St. Andrew. From there, they spread out so that there are now 25 Salesian centers along the western seaboard from Texas and New Mexico in the south to Edmonton, Canada in the north.

Around the beginning of the 20th century, adventurous Europeans, contrasting their lot with the fabulous tales of wealth coming from across the sea, eagerly pulled up stakes to seek their fortune in the New World. They poured into this country in droves from Scandinavia and the Baltic states, from Ireland and Scotland, from Italy and Germany and from half a dozen other nations. The masses were on the move!

Yet, as attractive as it was, Manhattan's churning melting pot was fraught with dangers for the faithful. Far from the old country, perplexed by the language barrier, there was a growing tendency among the newcomers to stray from the fold. Small wonder that the bishops and pastors became alarmed about the religious welfare of the immigrants. Thus, the call went out to the mother countries for help. For the Italians, Bishop Michael Corrigan sent an urgent appeal to the Superior General of the Salesians, and characteristically, Father Rua rose to the occasion.

By November of 1898, a band of Salesians, led by Father Ernest Coppo, later to become a Bishop, took over the Italian mission in the basement of old St. Brigid's and began canvassing among the east side dock workers and fruit vendors of Greenwich Village for parishioners. The simple answer to relieve the current crisis called for an all-out effort to uplift their fellow countrymen. The sons of Don Bosco plunged into this new venture with such wholehearted enthusiasm that their record is a shining tribute to their zeal for the salvation of souls. The Province of St. Philip was born.

In the year 1903, the opportunity presented itself to expand and develop the "infant province." It came about in this way: the diocesan seminary of Albany, located at Troy, was moved elsewhere and the buildings were turned over to the Salesians, who started a boarding school for boys. Five years later, this school was transferred to Hawthorne, where it remained till a fire destroyed the building in 1917. Meanwhile, another parish had been opened in New York City, that of Mary Help of Christians on 12th Street. This was followed by one in Paterson, N.J. and one in Port

Chester, N.Y. Then came two boarding schools: one at Ramsey, N.J., the other at New Rochelle, N.Y. Next came a parish in Elizabeth, N.J., then a boarding school at Goshen, N.Y. After that, the major seminary was established at Don Bosco College in Newton, N.J., while Mary, Help of Christians School was built at Tampa, Florida.

This all took place before 1930. Fifteen years were to elapse before another foundation would be made. Nevertheless, the Salesians never lost sight of the prophecies and predictions of their holy founder. They firmly believed that "in due time," they themselves would become a part of the visioned triumphs. As a result, the 15-year interim between 1930 and 1945 found them hard at work recruiting new blood—training a corps of personnel according to the exacting standards of the Preventive System, Don Bosco's particular method of educating the young, and supplying the lifeline for that surge of progress that was to come. Consequently, when the hour of Providence did dawn, the headquarters for the Province of St. Philip was on a firm footing in the Archdiocese of New York.

The Society's sudden awakening to a vigorous new life in the United States was a new wonder in its history. Initially, this was due to the pent-up need created by World War II. And who could not see the connecting link with Don

Bosco's dream? The quickening pace of the departure from pioneer days came in 1945, and Boston was its rallying cry. After Boston came other foundations in rapid succession, so that today the Eastern Province numbers 30 centers.

Decades have passed since the opening in Boston ushered in the boom era. Yet current facts and figures happily show that the Salesians have moved ahead even further. For example, Massachusetts and New Jersey each boast four establishments. Five new centers have blossomed in Canada, while Alabama, Louisiana, Florida, Illinois and Indiana now claim one each.

In the dream of Don Bosco, we saw a vast multitude of boys extending to the farthest horizon of the world. On his arrival in their midst, the boys approached, applauding him as though they had long been expecting him. He did not know them, but they knew him, as millions of boys today know him as their spiritual father. His guide had said, "You will understand everything in due time." That dream of Don Bosco began to take shape even before he died in 1888. Each year it continues to unfold itself further, and it is already marvellous in our eyes as it rolls into the future.

If you have enjoyed this book, consider making your next selection from among the following . . .

St. Monica. *F. A. Forbes*. 6.00
Pope St. Pius X. *F. A. Forbes* 8.00
The Guardian Angels 2.00
Eucharistic Miracles. *Joan Carroll Cruz* 15.00
The Incorruptibles. *Joan Carroll Cruz* 13.50
Padre Pio—The Stigmatist. *Fr. Charles Carty* 15.00
Ven. Francisco Marto of Fatima. *Cirrincione,* comp. 1.50
The Facts About Luther. *Msgr. P. O'Hare* 16.50
Little Catechism of the Curé of Ars. *St. John Vianney* . . 6.00
The Curé of Ars—Patron St. of Parish Priests. *O'Brien*. . 5.50
The Four Last Things: Death, Judgment, Hell, Heaven . . 7.00
St. Alphonsus Liguori. *Frs. Miller & Aubin* 16.50
Confession of a Roman Catholic. *Paul Whitcomb*. 1.50
The Catholic Church Has the Answer. *Paul Whitcomb*. . . 1.50
The Sinner's Guide. *Ven. Louis of Granada* 12.00
True Devotion to Mary. *St. Louis De Montfort* 8.00
Life of St. Anthony Mary Claret. *Fanchón Royer*. 15.00
Autobiography of St. Anthony Mary Claret 13.00
I Wait for You. *Sr. Josefa Menendez* 75
Words of Love. *Menendez, Betrone, Mary of the Trinity* . 6.00
Little Lives of the Great Saints. *John O'Kane Murray* . . 18.00
Prayer—The Key to Salvation. *Fr. Michael Müller* 7.50
The Victories of the Martyrs. *St. Alphonsus Liguori* 10.00
Canons and Decrees of the Council of Trent. *Schroeder* . 15.00
Sermons of St. Alphonsus Liguori for Every Sunday . . . 16.50
A Catechism of Modernism. *Fr. J. B. Lemius* 5.00
Alexandrina—The Agony and the Glory. *Johnston* 6.00
Life of Blessed Margaret of Castello. *Fr. Bonniwell* 7.50
The Ways of Mental Prayer. *Dom Vitalis Lehodey* 14.00
Fr. Paul of Moll. *van Speybrouck* 12.50
The Story of the Church. *Johnson, Hannan, Dominica* . . 16.50
Hell Quizzes. *Radio Replies Press*. 1.50
Purgatory Quizzes. *Radio Replies Press* 1.50
Virgin and Statue Worship Quizzes. *Radio Replies Press* . 1.50
Moments Divine before/Bl. Sacr. *Reuter* 8.50
Meditation Prayer on Mary Immaculate. *Padre Pio* 1.50
Little Book of the Work of Infinite Love. *de la Touche*. . 3.00
Textual Concordance of/Holy Scriptures. *Williams. Pb.* . . 35.00
Douay-Rheims Bible. *Paperbound* 35.00
The Way of Divine Love. (pocket, unabr.). *Menendez* . . . 8.50
Mystical City of God—Abridged. *Ven. Mary of Agreda*. . 18.50

Prices subject to change.

St. Teresa of Avila. *F. A. Forbes* 6.00
St. Vincent de Paul. *F. A. Forbes* 6.00
St. Ignatius Loyola. *F. A. Forbes* 6.00
St. Catherine of Siena. *F. A. Forbes* 6.00
St. Athanasius. *F. A. Forbes* 6.00
Set of 5 F. A. Forbes Saints' Lives 20.00
Stories of Padre Pio. *Tangari* 8.00
Miraculous Images of Our Lady. *Joan Carroll Cruz* 20.00
Miraculous Images of Our Lord. *Cruz* 13.50
Brief Catechism for Adults. *Fr. Cogan* 9.00
Raised from the Dead. *Fr. Hebert* 16.50
Autobiography of St. Margaret Mary 6.00
Thoughts and Sayings of St. Margaret Mary 5.00
The Voice of the Saints. *Comp. by Francis Johnston* . . . 7.00
The 12 Steps to Holiness and Salvation. *St. Alphonsus* . . 7.50
The Rosary and the Crisis of Faith. *Cirrincione/Nelson* . . 2.00
Dialogue of St. Catherine of Siena. *Transl. Thorold* 10.00
Catholic Answer to Jehovah's Witnesses. *D'Angelo.* 12.00
Twelve Promises of the Sacred Heart. (100 cards) 5.00
The Love of Mary. *D. Roberto* 8.00
Begone Satan. *Fr. Vogl* 3.00
St. Therese, The Little Flower. *John Beevers* 6.00
Mary, The Second Eve. *Cardinal Newman* 3.00
Devotion to Infant Jesus of Prague. *Booklet* 75
The Wonder of Guadalupe. *Francis Johnston* 7.50
Apologetics. *Msgr. Paul Glenn* 10.00
Baltimore Catechism No. 1 . . . . 3.50
Baltimore Catechism No. 2 . . . . 4.50
Baltimore Catechism No. 3 . . . . 8.00
An Explanation of the Baltimore Catechism. *Kinkead* . . . 16.50
Bible History. *Schuster* 13.50
Blessed Eucharist. *Fr. Mueller* 9.00
Catholic Catechism. *Fr. Faerber* 7.00
The Devil. *Fr. Delaporte* 6.00
Dogmatic Theology for the Laity. *Fr. Premm* 20.00
Evidence of Satan in the Modern World. *Cristiani* 10.00
Fifteen Promises of Mary. (100 cards) 5.00
Life of Anne Catherine Emmerich. 2 vols. *Schmoeger* . . . 37.50
Life of the Blessed Virgin Mary. *Emmerich* 16.50
Prayer to St. Michael. (100 leaflets) 5.00
Preparation for Death. (Abridged). *St. Alphonsus* 8.00
Purgatory Explained. *Schouppe* 13.50
Purgatory Explained. (pocket, unabr.). *Schouppe* 9.00
Trustful Surrender to Divine Providence. *Bl. Claude* 5.00

Prices subject to change.

Forty Dreams of St. John Bosco. *Bosco* 12.50
Blessed Miguel Pro. *Ball* 6.00
Soul Sanctified. *Anonymous* 9.00
Wife, Mother and Mystic. *Bessieres* 8.00
The Agony of Jesus. *Padre Pio*. 2.00
Catholic Home Schooling. *Mary Kay Clark* 18.00
The Cath. Religion—Illus. & Expl. *Msgr. Burbach* 9.00
Wonders of the Holy Name. *Fr. O'Sullivan* 1.50
How Christ Said the First Mass. *Fr. Meagher*. 18.50
Too Busy for God? Think Again! *D'Angelo* 5.00
St. Bernadette Soubirous. *Trochu*. 18.50
Passion and Death of Jesus Christ. *Liguori* 10.00
Life Everlasting. *Garrigou-Lagrange*. 13.50
Confession Quizzes. *Radio Replies Press*. 1.50
St. Philip Neri. *Fr. V. J. Matthews* 5.50
St. Louise de Marillac. *Sr. Vincent Regnault*. 6.00
The Old World and America. *Rev. Philip Furlong* 18.00
Prophecy for Today. *Edward Connor* 5.50
Bethlehem. *Fr. Faber* 18.00
The Book of Infinite Love. *Mother de la Touche*. 5.00
The Church Teaches. *Church Documents* 16.50
Conversation with Christ. *Peter T. Rohrbach*. 10.00
Purgatory and Heaven. *J. P. Arendzen*. 5.00
Liberalism Is a Sin. *Sarda y Salvany* 7.50
Spiritual Legacy/Sr. Mary of Trinity. *van den Broek*. . . . 10.00
The Creator and the Creature. *Fr. Frederick Faber*. 16.50
Radio Replies. 3 Vols. *Frs. Rumble and Carty* 42.00
Convert's Catechism of Catholic Doctrine. *Geiermann*. . . 3.00
Incarnation, Birth, Infancy of Jesus Christ. *Liguori* 10.00
Light and Peace. *Fr. R. P. Quadrupani* 7.00
Dogmatic Canons & Decrees of Trent, Vat. I 9.50
The Evolution Hoax Exposed. *A. N. Field* 7.50
The Priest, the Man of God. *St. Joseph Cafasso* 13.50
Christ Denied. *Fr. Paul Wickens* 2.50
New Regulations on Indulgences. *Fr. Winfrid Herbst*. . . . 2.50
A Tour of the Summa. *Msgr. Paul Glenn* 18.00
Spiritual Conferences. *Fr. Frederick Faber* 15.00
Bible Quizzes. *Radio Replies Press* 1.50
Marriage Quizzes. *Radio Replies Press*. 1.50
True Church Quizzes. *Radio Replies Press*. 1.50
Mary, Mother of the Church. *Church Documents* 4.00
The Sacred Heart and the Priesthood. *de la Touche* 9.00
Blessed Sacrament. *Fr. Faber*. 18.50
Revelations of St. Bridget. *St. Bridget of Sweden* 3.00

Prices subject to change.

Story of a Soul. *St. Therese of Lisieux* 8.00
Catholic Children's Treasure Box Books 1-10 . . . . 35.00
Prayers and Heavenly Promises. *Cruz* 5.00
Magnificent Prayers. *St. Bridget of Sweden* 2.00
The Happiness of Heaven. *Fr. J. Boudreau* 8.00
The Holy Eucharist—Our All. *Fr. Lucas Etlin* 2.00
The Glories of Mary. *St. Alphonsus Liguori* 16.50
The Curé D'Ars. *Abbé Francis Trochu* 21.50
Humility of Heart. *Fr. Cajetan da Bergamo* 8.50
Love, Peace and Joy. (St. Gertrude). *Prévot* 7.00
Père Lamy. *Biver* 12.00
Passion of Jesus & Its Hidden Meaning. *Groenings* 15.00
Mother of God & Her Glorious Feasts. *Fr. O'Laverty* . . . 10.00
Song of Songs—A Mystical Exposition. *Fr. Arintero* . . . 20.00
Love and Service of God, Infinite Love. *de la Touche* . . 12.50
Life & Work of Mother Louise Marg. *Fr. O'Connell.* . . . 12.50
Martyrs of the Coliseum. *O'Reilly* 18.50
Rhine Flows into the Tiber. *Fr. Wiltgen* 15.00
What Catholics Believe. *Fr. Lawrence Lovasik* 5.00
Who Is Therese Neumann? *Fr. Charles Carty* 2.00
Summa of the Christian Life. 3 Vols. *Granada* 36.00
St. Francis of Paola. *Simi and Segreti.* 8.00
The Rosary in Action. *John Johnson* 9.00
St. Dominic. *Sr. Mary Jean Dorcy.* 10.00
Is It a Saint's Name? *Fr. William Dunne* 2.50
St. Martin de Porres. *Giuliana Cavallini* 12.50
Douay-Rheims New Testament. *Paperbound* 15.00
St. Catherine of Siena. *Alice Curtayne* 13.50
Blessed Virgin Mary. *Liguori* 6.00
Chats With Converts. *Fr. M. D. Forrest* 10.00
The Stigmata and Modern Science. *Fr. Charles Carty* . . . 1.50
St. Gertrude the Great 1.50
Thirty Favorite Novenas 75
Brief Life of Christ. *Fr. Rumble* 2.00
Catechism of Mental Prayer. *Msgr. Simler* 2.00
On Freemasonry. *Pope Leo XIII* 1.50
Thoughts of the Curé D'Ars. *St. John Vianney* 2.00
Incredible Creed of Jehovah Witnesses. *Fr. Rumble* . . . 1.50
St. Pius V—His Life, Times, Miracles. *Anderson.* 5.00
St. Dominic's Family. *Sr. Mary Jean Dorcy* 24.00
St. Rose of Lima. *Sr. Alphonsus* 15.00
Latin Grammar. *Scanlon & Scanlon* 16.50
Second Latin. *Scanlon & Scanlon* 12.00
St. Joseph of Copertino. *Pastrovicchi* 6.00

Prices subject to change.

Saint Michael and the Angels. *Approved Sources* 7.00
Dolorous Passion of Our Lord. *Anne C. Emmerich* 16.50
Our Lady of Fatima's Peace Plan from Heaven. *Booklet* . .75
Three Ways of the Spiritual Life. *Garrigou-Lagrange* . . . 6.00
Mystical Evolution. 2 Vols. *Fr. Arintero, O.P.* 36.00
St. Catherine Labouré of the Mirac. Medal. *Fr. Dirvin* . . 13.50
Manual of Practical Devotion to St. Joseph. *Patrignani* . . 15.00
The Active Catholic. *Fr. Palau* 7.00
Ven. Jacinta Marto of Fatima. *Cirrincione* 2.00
Reign of Christ the King. *Davies* 1.25
St. Teresa of Avila. *William Thomas Walsh* 21.50
Isabella of Spain—The Last Crusader. *Wm. T. Walsh* . . . 20.00
Characters of the Inquisition. *Wm. T. Walsh* 15.00
Philip II. *William Thomas Walsh.* HB. 37.50
Blood-Drenched Altars—Cath. Comment. Hist. Mexico . . 20.00
Self-Abandonment to Divine Providence. *de Caussade* . . 18.00
Way of the Cross. *Liguorian* 1.00
Way of the Cross. *Franciscan* 1.00
Modern Saints—Their Lives & Faces, Bk. 1. *Ann Ball* . . 18.00
Modern Saints—Their Lives & Faces, Bk. 2. *Ann Ball.* . . 20.00
Divine Favors Granted to St. Joseph. *Pere Binet* 5.00
St. Joseph Cafasso—Priest of the Gallows. *St. J. Bosco* . 5.00
Catechism of the Council of Trent. *McHugh/Callan* 24.00
Why Squander Illness? *Frs. Rumble & Carty* 2.50
Fatima—The Great Sign. *Francis Johnston.* 8.00
Heliotropium—Conformity of Human Will to Divine. . . . 13.00
Charity for the Suffering Souls. *Fr. John Nageleisen* . . . 16.50
Devotion to the Sacred Heart of Jesus. *Verheylezoon* . . . 15.00
Sermons on Prayer. *St. Francis de Sales* 4.00
Sermons on Our Lady. *St. Francis de Sales* 10.00
Sermons for Lent. *St. Francis de Sales* 12.00
Fundamentals of Catholic Dogma. *Ott* 21.00
Litany of the Blessed Virgin Mary. (100 cards) 5.00
Who Is Padre Pio? *Radio Replies Press* 2.00
Child's Bible History. *Knecht* 5.00
The Life of Christ. 4 Vols. H.B. *Anne C. Emmerich.* . . . 60.00
St. Anthony—The Wonder Worker of Padua. *Stoddard* . . 5.00
The Precious Blood. *Fr. Faber.* 13.50
The Holy Shroud & Four Visions. *Fr. O'Connell* 2.00
Clean Love in Courtship. *Fr. Lawrence Lovasik.* 2.50
The Secret of the Rosary. *St. Louis De Montfort* 5.00

At your Bookdealer or direct from the Publisher.
Call Toll Free 1-800-437-5876

Prices subject to change.

ABOUT THE AUTHOR

This book was authored by Mother Frances Alice Monica Forbes, a sister of the Society of the Sacred Heart, Scotland.

The future author was born on March 16, 1869 and was named Alice Forbes. Alice's mother died when she was a child, and her father became the dominant influence in her life, helping to form Alice's virile personality and great capacity for work. She was raised as a Presbyterian.

In 1900 Alice became a Catholic. The Real Presence in the Eucharist had been the big stumbling-block to her conversion, but one day she was hit by the literal truth of Our Lord's words: "This is My Body." Only a few months after her conversion, she entered the Society of the Sacred Heart, becoming a 31-year-old postulant. She seems to have received her vocation at her First Communion, when Our Lord kindled in her heart "the flame of an only love."

In the convent, Sister Forbes used her keen intelligence and strong will to make generously and completely the sacrifices that Our Lord asked of her each day. She put great store by the virtue of obedience. Much of the latter part of her life was spent in illness and suffering, yet she was always kind and uncomplaining—a charming person and a "gallant" soul. Throughout her sufferings the most important thing to her was the love of God. She died in 1936.

Mother Frances Alice Monica Forbes wrote many

ABOUT THE AUTHOR

books, including a series of interesting short lives of selected Saints called "Standard Bearers of the Faith." One of these books, that on Pope St. Pius X, was very highly regarded by Cardinal Merry del Val, who was a close friend of Pope Pius X.

Other works by Mother Frances Alice Monica Forbes include *St. Ignatius Loyola, St. John Bosco: Friend of Youth, St. Teresa, St. Columba, St. Monica, St. Athanasius, St. Catherine of Siena, St. Benedict, St. Hugh of Lincoln, The Gripfast Series of English Readers* and *The Gripfast Series of History Readers*, various plays, and a number of other books.

The above information is from the book *Mother F. A. Forbes: Religious of the Sacred Heart—Letters and Short Memoir*, by G. L. Sheil (London: The Catholic Book Club, 1948, by arrangement with Longmans, Green & Co., Ltd.).